I DON'T LIKE THAT MUSIC

Robert H. Mitchell

Code No. 1095

Hope Publishing Company
CAROL STREAM IL 60188

Foreword

Perhaps the most explosive issue in churches today is that of worship music styles. Many congregations are buzzing with anxious, fevered discussion of the subject. Others have already "divided" in order to meet the differing preferences of people, some by scheduling contrasting services at different hours, and others by establishing a second church at another location! In this book, my longtime friend Robert Mitchell has spoken to the situation in a very helpful way.

There is nothing explosive or self-serving in Bob's approach. Obviously, like all people, he has artistic preferences. But he is not hoping to manipulate the reader to an exclusive commitment to *his* preferred music style. Apparently he believes that the church today needs a reasonably-eclectic standard of worship expression. His effort, as in his earlier work, *Ministry and Music*, is thoroughly pastoral. He encourages complete openness on the part of all – full-time worship leaders and worshipers alike – in order that each individual church may continue to worship as a complete *body*, not a fragmented one.

Mitchell's view is both biblical and historical. We may guess that arguments about proper church music existed even in New

Testament times; is that possibly the reason why the Apostle Paul suggested an inclusive repertoire of "psalms, hymns, and spiritual songs"? This book reminds us also that the repeated conflicts that have occurred throughout history have often been based on the same recurring prejudices and misconceptions.

In chapters five, six, and seven, Bob Mitchell deals with the three types of material which he believes to be at the center of most discussions of this kind – pop music, ethnic (non-western) music, and traditional music (sometimes called "classical"). The first and last of these are generally agreed to be the "villains," the choice being determined by one's point of view. Christian music of non-western cultures is one of Bob's specialties, and the larger church is responding to this challenge by including examples in modern American hymnals. It is my own view that this new form offers one of the opportunities to neutralize aesthetic conflict in a congregation. Nobody argues that African-Americans, Koreans, or Colombian Indians should use North American church music styles, either traditional or pop. Perhaps the use of a "Latino" song in typical worship in Our Town, USA may encourage acceptance of another type of "Anglo" music preferred by others in the same congregation.

Will the book help to meet the challenge of our day? It could, if Mitchell's practical approaches to "bringing about change" are followed. It seems to me that the responsibility lies more with leadership than with typical church members. By virtue of training, they should be best equipped to understand the validity of the rationale presented here. If they share the author's warm concern for each member of the church, they will pray for the wisdom and patience to work it out in their own congregations.

Donald P. Hustad
Senior Professor of Church Music
Southern Baptist Theological Seminary
Louisville, KY

CONTENTS

FOREWORD 3

PREFACE 7

1. THE NATURE OF THE ISSUE 13

2. CHANGE 19
   Change is Painful 21
   Change is Inevitable 25
   Change is Valuable 28
   Change is Biblical 31
   Change in the Church 32

3. WHY DON'T I LIKE SOMETHING DIFFERENT? 35
   The Old Way is More Scriptural 36
   The Old Carries On Denominational Traditions 38
   The Old Music is Good Music 41
   The Old Ways are More Comfortable 48
   Fear of the "Different" 50

4. AN INTERLUDE 51

5. "POP" MUSIC AND THE CHURCH 55
   "It"s Secular, Not Sacred Music" 59
   "Pop Music is Compulsive" 60
   "It's Too Loud" 61
   "I Can't Understand the Words" 63
   "It Has Unchristian Associations" 64
   "This Music Is Not Good Music" 66
   "I Don't Like Such Music" 69

6. CHURCH MUSIC FROM THE NON-WESTERN WORLD 71
   The Church's Musical Tradition 72
   Changes in Attitude 73
   The Contemporary Situation 75

Is It Scriptural? 76
Is It Traditional? 78
Is It Good Music? 80
Is It Comfortable? 81

7. TRADITIONAL HYMNODY AS "THE NEW" 85
Memory and the Church 86
Scripture 87
Creeds and Confessions 87
Classical Liturgies 88
Classical Prayers 88
Theological and Devotional Writings 89
Classic Hymnody as the Church's Memory 90
A Stabilizing Influence 91
Shared Experience 92
Hymn Tinkering 98
Is It Biblical? 102
Is It Traditional? 103
Are They Good Texts and Tunes? 103
Are They Comfortable? 104

8. BRINGING ABOUT CHANGE 109
Ask "Why?" Before "How?" 110
Understanding Must Accompany Change 112
Connect With History 116
Provide a Familiar Reassuring Context 116
The "New" Must Be Well Executed 117
Change Will Not Always Be Acceptable 119
Change Involves Consensus 120
Change Involves Trust 122
Be Patient! 123

9. AGREE TO DISAGREE 125
The Nature of the Church Community 126
We are a Diverse Group 126
Christ Is The Head 127
The Unity of The Church 128
Seeking Our Sisters' And Brothers' Good 129

ENDNOTES 133

Preface

"When I go to worship I don't like some of the music! It's too loud (or too quiet), too familiar (unfamiliar), too fast (slow), too highbrow (simplistic), too contemporary (classical), too......" You can complete the possibilities of these familiar complaints.

Most of us have these feelings from time to time - some people have them much of the time. The issue here is the question of how we deal with such responses. If we don't like the music we may simply endure it. Eventually, we may move to another church having worship which seems to include music more to our liking. However, it is likely that we may carry such an attitude of intolerance into any other situation. The problem is not the music but the attitude itself. This is a book about attitudes.

It is appropriate to have preferences in the field of music. (For those who do not read this Preface I will say this repeatedly throughout the book). There is nothing wrong with enjoying some kinds of music more than others. That is a wonderful part of the uniqueness of each of us. The problem arises when we insist that we can worship only through music of our liking, and, indeed, that worship of our church should include only such music.

All music is intrinsically an expression of emotion. Thus, anything to do with music tends to heighten our emotional responses. Our musical likes and dislikes are close to the surface. We are aware of them and express them freely. This is less true concerning other aspects of worship. For that reason, this book deals with attitudes relating to the music of worship. However, there is more than music at stake. A critical attitude can find as its focus anything that takes place as a part of worship. It may be the preaching style or content; the way the service is ordered; the mode of announcements or prayer or receiving the offering; the presence or absence of ecclesiastical elements (robes, processionals, candles, etc.). I am calling into question the attitude that says "Unless things please me, I can not (will not?) worship".

This is not to suggest the abandonment of positive, critical evaluation and concern. Questions always need to be asked: "Why are we doing this?", "Is it being done as well as is possible?", "What are we failing to do that would be helpful and appropriate?".

My previous book, *Ministry and Music*, focused on the attitudes involved in the relationship between pastor and musician as worship leaders. By the time that book was finished, an inescapable consideration emerged for me. The attitudes of *all* who are engaged in common worship are important, not only those of the leaders. It is the common acceptance of the elements of the worship experience that must precede worship itself.

These words are addressed, then, to worship leaders, but beyond them, to all who worship. Public worship is, by definition, a corporate experience. It is the gathering of the People of God. Its focus is upon God, not upon those who lead the worship. These leaders are themselves worshipers whose task is to open the gate which leads to an awareness of God and then, to step out of the way so that all may enter in. How, then, may all of us approach and experience public worship? What are the feelings within us that may get in the way of an encounter with God? Conversely, how can we come with an expectant, accepting attitude which allows God to speak?

My purpose, then, is to suggest that there are good reasons why one should attempt to understand, accept and enter into a variety of kinds of worship. These may include experiences which are not initially pleasant or comfortable.

There are a number of factors which are involved in this process. We will be considering such questions as:

- How did we form our present preferences?

- What is the rationale that sustains them?

- Why should we seek to change or expand them?

- How can we change them?

We need to learn how to become more acceptant of those things which do not immediately please us. God invites each of us into a variety of life experiences beyond those which we can presently comprehend and enjoy.

This book is offered to all who worship God as revealed in Jesus Christ. It seeks to engage all who desire and expect to experience a heightened awareness of God's Holy Spirit as they worship "in spirit and in truth".

I want to acknowledge my great indebtedness to the late Dr.

Erik Routley whose thoughts have stimulated so many of my own. I also want to recognize the many contributions made by my wife as well as family members, colleagues, and friends with whom I have discussed these sensitive matters for many years.

Robert H. Mitchell 1992

CHAPTER ONE

The Nature of the Issue

Each year, in the city of Edinburgh, Scotland, there is a world-famous festival of the arts. That festival traditionally begins with a worship service at St. Giles Cathedral.

Some years ago, the congregation at such a service included, as always, artists of the festival and civic leaders of Edinburgh. It was an elegant occasion. The colorful procession involved those with gold capes and swords, kilts, ermine and scarlet robes, top hats and white wigs, and a variety of rich ecclesiastical garments. The great organ shook the building. The preacher of the morning was Dr. Erik Routley. With great competence, the crimson-robed choir sang a very dissonant 12-tone anthem - a piece of music without friendly melody or familiar harmony. It was most appropriate for this occasion, in a context which focused on contemporary art. It was magnificently sung. After the service, at fellowship in St. Giles Hall, one of the civic leaders said "That was a great service, but I didn't care much for the choir music". Routley's response, "Bless your heart. You weren't supposed to *like* that anthem".

This rejoinder has some interesting implications. Is church music supposed to include only that which we like - or is worship - or preaching? Perhaps there is an occasional need for that which disturbs, startles, prods awake. Church music which is always familiar, pleasant and comfortable becomes unreal. C.S. Lewis has said about the nature of reality:

> ....nothing which is at all times and in every way agreeable to us can have objective reality. It is of the very nature of the real that it should have sharp corners and rough edges, that it should be resistant, should be itself. [1]

Sometimes the 'real' may need to intrude, even through the music, and even though it may not be comfortable. In the situation described above, the "sharp corners" and "rough edges" were apparent in the anthem. They served to communicate to some the reality of God's world today and the circumstances to which the Gospel was to be addressed by the artists.

This exemplifies a small part of the problem which every worship leader faces. Pastors and church musicians know that it is virtually impossible to choose worship music which appeals equally to every member of the congregation. Why is it that our musical appetites and expectations are so varied? In the example above of the Edinburgh worship service, the attitude of the civil servant suggests several conclusions on our part.

1. He expected worship music which was familiar and pleasant - and was disappointed.
2. He was probably unused to 12-tone music in any context.
3. He disliked and rejected the music he got.

This is an attempt to address the problem illustrated here. There are many reasons for disliking the music we encounter in worship. Sometimes music is disliked simply because it is insensitively chosen or ineptly performed by choir, soloist, organ or congregation. A pastor's comment, "The choir sang, after which worship was resumed" is a relevant one if the problem was simply that the choir sang badly. There are already many books which address the problems of poor choice and unmusical performance. We will not attempt to deal with these issues.

A more subtle and pervasive difficulty is encountered when worship music does not conform to expectations and desires of individual worshipers. In such a situation the attitudes of resentment and resistance may easily occur.

Our objective is to consider how we can deal with that which is perceived as being unfriendly or unpredictable - which is different from that which we have come to expect. Is there a need in worship for that which is new and therefore strange? If so, how do we reconcile that need with the opposite one - the need for that which is familiar, comforting and reassuring?

Certainly we cannot do without those familiar things which have come to symbolize our faith and Christian pilgrimage. Every community, Christian or non-Christian, develops expressions which symbolize its identity and purpose. These expressions must be maintained.

This is true of church music. Particularly in the free church, the music often functions as the primary, familiar liturgical structure. That is what we do every week which gives meaning and continuity to worship. This element of worship must be recognized, protected, nurtured and maintained.

However, an opposite dynamic is also present. "I know what I like!". That is often a way of saying "I like what I know!". Such a stance represents a commitment to the status quo and an attendant resistance to anything that might disturb it. In response to such resistance to anything new we need to ask, "How did we get this way?" and, "What might we do to expand appreciation and permit a richer, fresher experience of worship?"

A series of questions may be posed for all of us at this point.

How have you decided what you like in church music?

Why do you like those things that you enjoy?

Why do you feel that some pieces of music are "too old" or "too new" or "unchristian"?

In general, why do you think that some kinds of music are more appropriate than others?

Our attitudes toward church music are often formed and limited in ways of which we are quite unaware. Such formative influences deserve examination. It could be enlightening to discover:

What was the content and context of previous significant religious experiences? For example, such might characterized the particular meeting and community in which you first encountered Christ or made some commitment to Him and His Church.

What music characterized those situations in which you found teaching and help in growing toward Christian maturity? Are they to be normative for all future experiences?

What were the attitudes and teachings about music of Christian leaders whom you respected?

What are the boundaries of your non-church musical experiences? If you have never liked jazz or Mozart, it is unlikely that you will welcome them as a part of worship.

What was the musical environment in which you traditionally worshipped - perhaps from childhood?

What kinds of music do you associate with styles of Christian worship that you dislike?

All of these experiences may serve to create a feeling in us of what is "right" and what is "'wrong." Such feelings should not operate to limit our perceptions of how God can work through music. They need to be explored.

This book is about our attitudes concerning church music and worship. It seeks to explore reasons why we respond as we do. It examines those factors which generate and sustain our preferences and prejudices. It identifies factors which work to inhibit the change and growth which should characterize the maturing Christian and the developing life of the church.

We will look at Biblical teaching concerning the old and the new. We will examine historical and traditional elements which affect our attitude toward worship. We will consider some contemporary examples of the "new" which could serve to enrich our worship and our Christian understanding. We will consider the processes by means of which attitudes may be changed so that our Christian life can be enriched and its boundaries expanded.

Finally, we will examine the nature of the community which is the Church with the expectation that such examination may shed light on appropriate responses we might have.

Most of all, any such considerations must involve some kind of change on our part. Thus, our first discussion will deal with change and how we deal with it.

Let's return to the example given in the opening of this chapter. The 12-tone music was difficult for part of the congregation to understand. Should we intentionally use such things? Why? I would like to quote and paraphrase a passage from an article by

Gregory Wolfe.[2] In a book review he is dealing with the place of all of contemporary art in worship. I alter his words to focus on music.

The danger of distraction is real when inappropriate liturgical music is done in church (12-tone anthems?), but the opposite danger is music that does not challenge or awaken in the listener the continual surprises and paradoxes of the Christian message.

CHAPTER TWO

Change

"If you worship the same God today that you worshiped yesterday you are worshiping an idol!"

That seems like an outrageous statement. Is God not the same yesterday, today and forever? Is He not "Our help in ages past, our hope for years to come, and our eternal home"? Of course!

An idol is a representation of God which is, itself, revered or worshiped. It can be carved of stone. It can be painted on wood as were medieval icons. It can be constructed in the mind as a collection of ideas which define the god whom we worship. Whether it is a carving, a painting, or a cluster of ideas, it is only a representation, not the real thing. No human being is able to contain the Almighty God in any such form.

In the theology of icons, it is made very clear that these pictures are only symbols to remind the worshiper of a Reality that lies beyond the images. C.S. Lewis has suggested that their function is to be as a window to look through, rather than to exist as an end in themselves. In his language, they are to be "permeable".[1] Unfortunately, throughout history icons have often become the subject of worship rather than the means by which one is aided in worship of the true God.

The same may happen with words and ideas. A collection of words (the Bible) can be worshiped as being the "holy" itself, though it is God alone who is holy. A collection of ideas about God, Jesus Christ, and salvation is called a "theology". Unfortunately, such a construct of human words and ideas can be invested with His attributes of being eternal, unchangeable, absolute. When this happens, these words and ideas have become a substitute for Him - thus, an idol.

Now consider the statement made at the beginning of this chapter. It is not a description of God but a comment about each one of us. It would be equally outrageous to say "I now know everything that there is to know about God". The Maker of the universe, the great "I Am" cannot be imprisoned in the limitations of our thoughts and experiences. There is always more for us to know about God. When we refuse new understanding, it can be truly said that we worship not the living God but an unchangeable idol made of our past experience. This is true about all Christian understanding. At this point, it is relevant that such can be true about our attitudes toward church music.

The whole idea of new experience implies change. Change and growth are linked together. God invites us to new, richer, fuller understanding and appreciation of Him, His world, and His will for our lives - including our worship. That is our focus.

CHANGE
IS PAINFUL

People don't usually welcome change, especially in church music and worship. When we consider change in relationship to church music and liturgy we have a problem. One very valid aspect of worship is that of providing a stable, predictable, reassuring element in our lives. However, we tend to become captive to this expectation and do not want it to be questioned. There has always been resistance to the changing of familiar worship experiences.

When the 16th century Protestant Reformation took place in England, many things happened which seem good to us from our 20th century vantage point. Preaching was restored to a place of importance. Congregational singing (Psalms) was made a part of worship for the first time in many centuries. The Scriptures were heard in English - the common language. But in 1549, in England, the commoners of Devonshire and Cornwall submitted 15 articles to the king. They read, in part:

> Item, we will not receive the new service because it is but like a Christmas game, but we will have our old service of matins, mass, even song, and procession in Latin and not in English, as it was before. [2]

It did not matter that the new service made it possible for them to understand, participate and be instructed. Against all this was the intolerable fact that their worship had been changed.

In the 1960s changes similar to those of the 16th century were made in Roman Catholic worship by the Second Vatican Council. Many of us remember the outrage with which change from Latin to English was received by many sincere Catholic worshipers. In the fall of 1967, Time magazine reported an incident in St. Louis where a Roman Catholic family was charged with disturbing the peace. They insisted on shouting out the old Latin words of worship in the midst of the new vernacular service.

Again, in Time magazine of April 26, 1976, we read in one of the letters to the editor:

> The decline, if one may call it that, of Roman Catholicism is due mainly to the hucksterism of pastors and bishops who engineered the "liberalism" of the mass. Banjo plucking, guitar strumming, and folk singing added to the switch from Latin and the reversal of the altar have disenchanted thousands of Catholics. While these machinations may appeal to the young, they frustrate the older people who pay the freight.

For another example, consider the emotional responses by many to the new versions of scripture which began to emerge in the middle of the 20th century. Objections were made, saying in effect, "Certainly the King James Bible is the true scripture and is proper for worship".

A rather amusing parallel may still be found in older copies of the King James Bibles which contain in the front not only a dedication to King James, but also a "Preface to the Readers".

In this preface, the translators are pleading for patience and acceptance on the part of the readers. There was apparently much resistance to this "new" version (1611). The preface says in part:

> ....(this translation) deserveth much respect and esteem, but yet findeth cold entertainment in the world. It is welcomed with suspicion instead of love....For was there ever anything of newness or renewing, but the same endured many a storm of gainsaying or opposition.

Dr. Hugh Broughton, a distinguished 17th century British Latin, Greek, and Hebrew scholar had this to say about the new "King James" version:

> (The Authorized Version) was sent to me to censure: which bred in me a sadness which will grieve me while I breath, it is so ill done. Tell his Majesty that I would rather be rent in pieces by wild horses, then that any such translation by my consent should be urged upon the poor churches...The cockles of the seashores, and the leaves of the forest, and the grains of the poppy may as well be numbered as the gross errors of this Bible.[3]

Remember, the time is the 1600s. People in that day had as much difficulty accepting a new version of scripture (the King James Bible) as many earnest Christians do today.

A third example, this time in the field of church music, has to do with an attempt in 18th century America to teach church people to read music. At that time, if the ordinary parishioner had a hymn book at all, it usually contained only words. In many churches, the text was "lined out" by a deacon or precenter. That is, he would sing one phrase alone, after which the congregation would then repeat it. The next phrase would follow in similar fashion until the hymn or psalm was completely sung. Some thought that singing in worship would be more musical and satisfying if members of the congregation could learn to read music. This was the beginning of the "singing schools".

Immediately, Christians were divided as to whether the "old way" or the "new way" (reading music) was proper. The controversy became a heated one. Sermons were preached and tracts written advocating one side or the other.

In 1712 a tract was written addressing this subject by Rev. Thomas Symmes of Bradford, Massachusetts who was in favor of the "new way". In this, he published a list of objections to the new way "which had reached his ears". He listed ten of these:

1. It is a new way, an unknown tongue.

2. It is not so melodious as the usual way.

3. There are so many tunes that we shall never have done learning them.

4. The practice creates disturbances, and causes people to behave indecently and disorderly.

5. It is Quakerish and Popish and introductive of instrumental music. [Note that neither the Catholics, (the "Popish"), nor the Quakers used congregational music in their regular service sat that time. It was considered "fair game" to charge these groups of "outsiders" with anything which might be controversial for the orthodox Christian].

6. The names given to the notes ["do, re, mi", etc] are bawdy, yea blasphemous.

7. It is a needless way since our fathers got to heaven without it.

8. It is a contrivance to get money.

9. People spend too much time learning it, they tarry out nights disorderly.

10. They are a company of young upstarts that fall in with this way, and some of them are lewd and loose persons.[4]

Many of these 18th century objections to something new in the church have a familiar ring to us today. Some of them are still used to express objections to the "new". People simply do not want change which affects their worship and its music. They will offer any excuse, no matter how unreasonable, to avoid it.

A comment tempering the above needs to be made. Of course some change, obviously for the better, is welcomed. Such welcome may be ambivalent, regretting that which is gone at the same time as affirming that which is new. A key to dealing with this is the recognition of the biblical truth that one can look for "God working in all things for good". [Rom. 8:28]

CHANGE
IS INEVITABLE

In the cathedral of Cologne, Germany, the visitor may pay a small charge and descend the steps to a room under the nave and see the riches of the "Treasury". There one finds the things of medieval worship - elaborate gold crosses, reliquaries, bishop's crosiers, and similar items from medieval times. Included among these are some bishop's copes. The cope was a kind of short cape, worn for high moments of worship. One particular cope on display is made of cloth of gold and weighs over 40 pounds.

At the time of the Protestant Reformation, many of the reformers protested the use of such elaborate and expensive garments for worship. Two of those who objected, John Calvin and John Knox, were university lecturers. They said, in effect, "We will wear our ordinary working clothes into the pulpit rather than these costly robes". What were their working business suits? A black robe with white tabs at the collar. Today, this clothing which was worn initially to protest the use of special garments by the clergy has become just that - special garments for the preacher or worship leader. The point here is not to discuss the appropriateness of special clerical garb. Rather, it is to suggest that the meaning of these garments has changed while they have remained the same. As the church conserves what it has and does, the meanings attached to these things will inevitably be altered.

In the case of congregational music, there has been a continuing pattern of such change. In the 16th century in the Lutheran reformation, congregational hymns were introduced into worship. Since there was no existing form of song for the congregation to use in the celebration of the Mass, new musical expressions needed to be developed. Therefore, Martin Luther and others wrote new texts and used for their music an idiom which was more like the tavern songs of the day. It had no resemblance to the Gregorian chant or choral polyphonic music which the choirs of monks had been singing. This new idiom was perceived as being very "secular" in its own time. However, today, these same German chorale tunes (many of them altered by Bach) have become the epitome of "sacred" music. As colloquial musical styles changed, this music, conserved by the church, has come to symbolize something quite different from its original associations.

For example, the familiar passion chorale, the musical setting for "O Sacred Head Now Wounded" has become for us the essence of Christian music. No ordinary worshiper thinks of connecting it with its original love song text "My Heart Was Wounded for the Love of a Fair Maiden". This was its association in earlier days. The passage of time and the development of new associations has brought about a change of meaning.

In the case of 16th century Calvinistic music, the tunes of the new metrical psalms which he used seemed inappropriate to many. Queen Elizabeth referred to them as "Geneva Jigs" and Shakespear commented on the Genevan practice of "singing songs to hornpipes". Today, it is hard for us to comprehend this attitude. To us, nothing sounds less like dance music than the tune "Old Hundredth" which was the setting for Psalm 134 in Calvin's *Geneva Psalter* and which we use to sing Psalm 100 or the familiar doxology "Praise God From Whom All Blessings Flow". A drastic but unplanned change of meaning has taken place across the years.

The 19th century gospel song has become the world-wide expression of evangelical Christianity. Today, we are not aware that its musical roots are in the idiom of popular parlor music of a century ago. This relationship contributed to its great usefulness in mass evangelism of the later part of the 19th century. However, popular music has changed since then, and that which once had a strong "secular" connotation has now become a "sacred" musical idiom.

In this century, there was great objection to some of the tunes used by Ralph Vaughn Williams in the English Hymnal of 1906. An example would be the tune "Sine Nomine" which was used with the text "For All The Saints". Such tunes were viewed by some contemporaries as "jazz".

Today it is difficult for many to remember the shock and offense which came with the introduction of new forms of church music beginning in the 1960s. "Pop" music invaded the church, with musicals for youth, drums, guitars, and other "secular" instruments intruding into our worship. Today, however, in many churches these sounds have become quite normal and acceptable. Full orchestras (often on tape) accompany singers and choirs in churches where, just a few decades ago, the only acceptable instruments were organ and piano.

More to the point, much of such music, whether in the sanctuary or as part of TV's electronic gospel presentations, is becoming instantly recognizable as being "religious" music. The radical discontinuity of "new" church music with the expectations of the church is gradually changing to an acceptance of it as a normal expression of Christian worship and witness.

In each of the above examples, the same process has been at work. Traditional church music, of any period, has been a specialized, esoteric kind of expression. Circumstances have operated to introduce some new idiom - one which comes from the secular world outside of the church. That new idiom has always met scorn and rejection on the part of some within the church. However, the pattern is repeated historically, and over a period of time the "new" idiom has become a part of the distinctive cultic musical expression of the church.

As long as the church exists in a changing society, it is inevitable that the meaning of that which it maintains will change in relationship to the society around it. Thus, change simply cannot be halted - to change nothing is to change.

Growth which involves change is often painful. In some of the phrases from a song of a few years ago which speaks of both change and pain:

> Without clouds the rain can't wash the land.
> Never took a journey and not leave some place behind.
> Without pain the joy in life won't show.[5]

CHANGE
IS VALUABLE

We need change. Earlier, I have mentioned the value of worship as it contains that which is predictable, reassuring, comfortable. While true, all of this may also have a dysfunctional aspect. Things can become so familiar that they no longer register upon our consciousness. A prayer may be uttered or a hymn sung so many times in a familiar, unchanging context that they become simply repetition by rote. We can set our mouth to singing an over- familiar hymn and mentally go off and leave it running. Our conscious assent to the propositions expressed is no longer present; our engagement with the commitments which are made in the hymn is absent. The 19th century English pastor and author, George MacDonald expressed this problem as he said "Nothing is so deadening to the divine as an habitual dealing with the outsides of holy things".[6]

The Jewish philosopher Abraham Heschel spoke of the difficulty we are considering in this way:

> The power of being human is easily dissolved in the process of excessive trivialization. Banality and triteness, the by-products of repetitiveness, continue to strangle or corrode the sense of significant being. Boredom is a spiritual disease, infectious and deadening, but cureable[7]

While he is speaking of all of life's experiences, this certainly describes the boring dullness that can take place in worship.

Eugene Nida of the American Bible Society comments on this matter of familiarity and predictability. He uses the term "information" to describe "data which registers at a deep motivating level". This concerns that which reaches us effectively, and involves our attitudes and values - certainly a concern central to the objectives of Christian worship. He says in his book *Message and Mission:*

> A fundamental principle of information theory is that the amount of "information" carried by any item is directly proportionate to its unpredictability. In other words, if we can predict the occurrence of a particular word or expression, then that word carries very little "information" or impact.[8]

Although he is speaking of the problem of the translation of scripture, the principle involved is relevant for our consideration of worship and its music. The more predictable it is, the less impact it will have on our consciousness.

Speaking of the music of the choir in worship, Archibald Davison offers a devastating comment. He suggests that:

> ....for most laymen, Sunday's music has no greater meaning than that of a more or less agreeable or disagreeable interruption of the service.[9]

Continuing, he categorizes these agreeable or disagreeable interruptions of the service as being active or passive. Concerning the active agreeable interruptions, he suggests:

> ..among active agreeable interruptions are those anthems which by reason of some associations rouse the worshiper to placid recognition of the fact that a particularly welcome musical acquaintance is present; at some time a nice tune in it, or the way it was sung caught the layman's fancy; repeated hearings have enabled him to recognize this piece and perhaps even call it by name. So, all in all, he would say that it was one of his favorites.

He describes a passive musical interruption this way:

> A passive musical interruption is represented by one of a group of old and accepted musical associates, though not necessarily a favorite, which tells the same threadbare story it has told any number of times before, a narrative cast in words of one syllable, so familiar that only a tolerant awareness of the telling is required. To anthems like this the layman clings lovingly and with a loyalty that is stubborn and almost maternal. Their presence, to be sure, makes no greater impact than the ringing of the church bell or the presence of the pulpit, and their familiarity is, to borrow an expression of D. W. Prall, no more than inattentively felt dullness.

All of these men are expressing in one way or another the fact that change or some kind of newness is important for meaningful worship.

CHANGE
IS BIBLICAL

In several of the Psalms, we read the admonition "sing a new song unto the Lord". [Psalms 33, 90, 98, 144, 149]. Then the psalmist goes on to rehearse the familiar stories of the mighty acts of God. God remains the same, but we are to sing about His greatness in new ways. What was wrong with the old songs which told the same story? Perhaps the same human tendency to become hardened and oblivious to the familiar. So the psalmist says "I will sing a new song to thee, O God" [Psalm 124]. Something new has happened: some new insight into God's way of dealing with us: some new awareness of His goodness; some new challenge to our way of life. Thus God becomes new to us and our song must find a way to express this new appreciation and understanding of Him.

In the New Testament, Jesus confronts His religious peers with change. The law is reinterpreted [e.g. Matt. 9]. Worship is viewed in a new context [Matt. 5, John 4]. At the Last Supper, Jesus suggests that God's covenant with us has become a new one. He summarizes this in a statement to the disciples where He says, "Therefore, every scribe who has been trained for the kingdom of heaven is like a householder who brings out of his treasures what is new and what is old." [Matt 13:52]. We are to have BOTH the new and the old in our worship.

The apostle Paul speaks of newness by using the image of "growing up" into Christ. In our own experience, we are familiar with the tragic situation in which a person fails to grow up mentally - where the body enlarges and matures but the mind remains that of an infant. No change takes place; no newness of understanding and appreciation develops. The person may appear mature, but the reality is that of a childish level of understanding.

In such a way, it is possible for growth and change to be absent from our spiritual lives. Thus the words of a preacher concerning a child who fell out of bed and said "I went to sleep too close to the place where I got in" express this common problem. We are all in danger of becoming too comfortable and of falling asleep too close to the point where we entered the Christian faith.

Paul speaks of the spiritual child who feeds on the milk of the Word as being a "babe in Christ". He uses this metaphor to suggest our need to progress to Christian adulthood through partaking of solid spiritual food [1 Cor. 3]. We find this idea used again in the fifth chapter of Hebrews. The point is simply that change must take place as one progresses from infancy to adulthood. In every person, this change involves feelings of struggle and resistance but it is a necessary part of growth into spiritual maturity. Thus change and newness need to be embraced rather than rejected. It is the way in which we enter into the fullness of life which God offers to us. This must take place in our music and worship as well as our understanding of Christian faith.

CHANGE
IN THE CHURCH

Concerning music in a particular congregation today, the "familiar" may be many things. It can be the classic sounds of Bach.

Palestrina, or Handel. It can be the romantic music of the late 19th - early 20th century - Shelley, Maunder, Noble, Buck. It may be the "contemporary" sound of the last 30 years - Peterson, Gaither. None of this music is bad. The "badness" lies in the assumption that this is all there is. Just as the preacher must attempt to preach the whole counsel of God, rather than limiting the sermon to a few contemporary or traditional insights, so the musician must recognize, affirm and try to use the wealth of variety of the Church's music, whether contemporary or classical. As musicians, we must be intentional about seeking to use "that which is old" and "that which is new".

A comment must be made concerning the possible unfavorable aspects of change. No matter how desirable and necessary, change will not always be an improvement. There can be unwanted consequences of seeking change itself. Some of these have been suggested. In addition, two other matters deserve attention.

First, to seek change may entice one into using things which are faddish but are not truly useful. To simply replace that which seems dull with something which is "with it" may be no real improvement. The embracing of novelty and cleverness for its own sake has no place in ministry.

Second, we must reconsider the 12-tone anthem which was used in Edinburgh and described at the beginning of Chapter 1. In that situation the attention of the service was focused on things which were on the growing edge of the arts. Many in the congregation would have been disappointed if the music did not reflect such a concern. That may not be true with your worshipers. The use of such an idiom must be weighed against Paul's admonitions concerning "speaking in unknown tongues" [1 Cor. 14]. Only those familiar with a specific individual situation can decide whether a certain musical expression can function usefully. The easy answer to this question is found in taking no risks. The more difficult one demands careful consideration as to whether possible values may outweigh negative response. If very few in the congregation are able to understand and enter into that which is done, it is dysfunctional and had better not be tried. Chapter 8 suggests some ways in which this problem may be dealt with. Nevertheless, we need to remember that living the Christian life always involves risk.

"If you worship the same God today that you worshiped yesterday, you are worshipping an idol". Paul, writing to the church at Ephesus, reminds them of the incompleteness of their knowledge and experience with these words:

> I pray that Christ will make his home in your hearts through faith. I pray that you may have your roots and foundations in love, so that you, together with all God's people may have the power to understand how broad and long, how high and deep, is Christ's love. Yes, may you come to know his love - although it can never be fully known - and so be completely filled with the very nature of God. [Eph. 3:17-19]

CHAPTER THREE

Why Don't I Like Something Different

Why do many churchgoers find change or newness in music or worship difficult to accept? How do they justify resistance to such change? Here are several factors which might be at work. These are some of the rationalizations which may be used to support the desire to cling to the old and reject the new.

THE OLD WAY
IS MORE SCRIPTURAL

Behind resistance to change often lies the assumption, usually unexamined, that there is a biblically "right" kind of church music and worship. This idea of "rightness" may be thought to be based upon the scriptural teaching concerning such matters. An examination of this foundational source provides information which might prove to be surprising.

Early on, it is important to be aware that the New Testament does not describe the proper or best kind of music for Christian worship. As Erik Routley suggested in response to the question as to whether jazz music is Christian, "No, it is not Christian, nor is any other kind of music".[1] The New Testament simply does not address this subject. Scripture is very clear in affirming the importance of congregational song - the expression of all believers.[2] It also has much to say about improper attitudes which can be involved in all Christian activity including the making of music (laziness, pride, self-serving, etc.). However, it makes no attempt to describe Christian music in musical terms. Chant? Metrical Psalms? Chorales? Hymns of human experience? American revival gospel songs? Black Gospel? Contemporary folk? Praise choruses? Heavy metal rock? All of these and many other musical styles have been used by the Church as appropriate expressions of its worship and fellowship. Which is right or wrong: which is best? The New Testament does not say.

The situation is made even more confusing by the fact that the New Testament also fails to include a clear and unambiguous description of just how Christian worship is to be ordered and experienced. Thus we have an enormous variety of worship forms and expectations within the history and present life of the Church. The many church listings found in the telephone directory of any large city (c. 31 columns in San Francisco) testify to the differences of understanding which are present. Many of these distinctions center in matters of public worship. Most of these views of the church and its worship claim to be rooted in the first and second century events as recorded in the New Testament and other early Christian writings. Yet think of their incredible variety and differences.

Consider the simplicity of the Quaker service; the profuse stimulation of Eastern Orthodox worship which involves all of the senses; evangelistic worship which focuses overtly on the personal appropriation of the death and resurrection of Jesus Christ; the historically rich Anglican liturgy; the charismatic Pentecostal experience with its high awareness of the immediate presence and working of God's Spirit. Is God better pleased with one or another of these forms or styles of worship? Of course not!

This is not to say that all worship is "Christian". There are very broad and basic principles found repeatedly in the scriptures:

- God is. He creates and sustains and loves all of life;
- Jesus Christ is the ultimate revelation of God for humanity;
- God's Spirit is His vital presence in today's world;
- The Scriptures are God's word to His people - and to all of the human race.

Even though a community may assent to the above statements, its worship, based upon them, may differ remarkably from that of another community. Such differences frequently find their foundation in a few carefully selected passages of scripture. (ignoring others) or in a tradition which originally had such a focus. Thus many communities can be said to have worship which is "scriptural" although the worship of each may differ radically from the other. To say "Our worship is scriptural" does not really settle anything. It may conform to certain passages of scripture.

So may many other forms.

Both the Old and the New Testament are clear that, ultimately, it is not the form of worship which is important but rather the attitude of heart on the part of the worshiper. We can understand this. However, such understanding does not really help the negative emotional reaction which we tend to have if we find ourselves in a worship experience which is substantially different from that to which we are accustomed. The argument that one kind of worship music is more "Scriptural" than another simply is not defensible when appealing to the Bible.

THE OLD CARRIES ON DENOMINATIONAL TRADITIONS

Some of this may be true. However, one should become familiar with one's denominational roots before assenting to such a proposition. For example, many of those in the Presbyterian and Reformed traditions might be surprised to learn that only in comparatively recent times have those groups sung anything but the words of scripture. - mainly the Psalms. Also, the use of any kind of musical instruments in worship was completely forbidden in the early days of these denominations. There were even struggles as to whether a pitch pipe was to be considered a musical instrument and thus forbidden.

For Baptists, at least those who trace their roots to the ministry of John Smythe in early seventeenth century England, changes have been even more radical. His church had prohibitions similar to those mentioned above against the use of instruments and the singing of anything but the Psalms. However, there were other restrictions. All singing was to be done from memory. Smythe wrote "I hold it to be unlawful to hold the book before the eye while singing".[3] Furthermore. only the males in the congregation were to sing.

Other restrictions were equally drastic. Only the baptized members of that particular local congregation were to join in the singing. After all, should not only the redeemed join in singing praise and prayers to their Lord? Anything else would be dishonest. Jesus said, quoting Isaiah, "This people serves me with their lips but their heart is far from me" (Matt. 15:8). How can we know the heart of the visitor with us? Thus, in the early 1600s a group of Baptist deacons from the London area were called to visit upon a neighboring congregation to get an explanation as to why they permitted "conjoint singing" - that is, allowing all present to join in the singing whether or not they were baptized members of the congregation.

There were good reasons for these concerns. This part of the Church was rebelling against the practices of the Anglican state religion. These reformers were attempting to uphold the principles that (l) women should keep silence in church (defended by a specific scriptural text), (2) that one could not truly mean what one was singing if the words were merely read from the page as in the Anglican Liturgy, not written on the heart, and (3) that the Church was composed of only those adult believers who had made a conscious commitment to the saving work of Christ. Therefore, only the Church should sing; who knew about all those other people?

Parenthetically, as is often the case, in at least one of these old concerns there is some valid truth which is applicable for us in our time. It is a frequently-heard lament of worship leaders that people often sing words of praise, testimony and commitment without really noticing what they are expressing. The 17th century problem of "just reciting words written on the page" is still with us. John Smythe's 17th century solution of "singing without the book before the eye" suggests one way of addressing this problem today. There are other possible solutions. Anytime one memorizes the text of a great hymn - makes it an indelible part of the furniture of one's mind, one has implanted a valuable resource for all seasons. The possibility of truly "singing with the spirit and with the understanding" can be greatly enhanced by committing the words of hymns to memory.

The earliest Baptist tradition concerning singing said; only Psalms, only men, only members, no books, no choir or instruments. It would be ridiculous to suggest that, in general, Baptist churches today are maintaining those old traditional ways of using music. It would be remarkable if they would want to. Nevertheless, these are Baptist roots and music traditions, and if we appeal to our history, this is what we mean. Of course, it is not what we want or expect today.

Another approach for Baptists might be to take late 19th century revivalism and evangelism as our model. Many believe that the Gospel Songs of Sankey, Bliss, Lowry, Crosby, and their contemporaries might be viewed as reflecting the true Baptist heritage. Let's look at this. The type of hymnal which emerged at the beginning of this tradition can be characterized by the Sankey/ Bliss *Gospel Hymns and Sacred Songs*, published in 1875. A little over half of these songs deal with personal salvation - encounter with Jesus, commitment to Him, and the hope of attaining heaven. However, the remainder includes metrical Psalms, hymns by Watts, Wesley, and other 18th century hymn writers. (There is nothing from the German or pre-Reformation traditions). The Sankey singing tradition itself was not limited to the use of Gospel Songs.

There was an earlier equally common Baptist singing tradition in the 18th century. The book most commonly published and used was some version of the *Psalms and Hymns of Isaac Watts* from early 18th century England. To say that the Gospel Song,

Watts, or the metrical Psalm represents the "old" Baptist tradition simply betrays a lack of knowledge of these and earlier Baptist practices. When we appeal to "tradition" we are frequently making uninformed choice of one among many traditions.

Before anyone of any denominational tradition suggests that present practice is simply the maintenance of the good old ways, he or she should discover just what those ways were. Therefore, to justify present practice (the familiar one) on the basis of historicity may be as misleading as the attempt to do so on the basis of explicit scriptural teaching.

THE OLD MUSIC
IS GOOD MUSIC

This statement opens up the issue of making value judgments in the fields of music and poetry. What do we mean when we say "good"?

It is easy and appropriate to say "I like that music". However, to affirm "That was good church music is a much more complex matter if that affirmation is to be a knowledgeable and thoughtful one. Upon what basis does one make this kind of value judgment?

To begin with, any value assessment in the field of music must deal with matters of musical craftsmanship and inspiration on the part of composer and performer. There are traditionally accepted rules of melodic structure, harmony and counterpoint. These are universal in the music of the Western world. They do not limit what the composer can do, but their violation must be a matter of intent, not ignorance. Consensus can generally be reached by those who have submitted to the study of these disciplines. One melody or harmonic structure can be judged to be better than another.

However, to follow all of the rules does not make a piece of music good - it may keep it from being bad. The element of imagination or artistic inspiration is also a relevant factor. This is more difficult to evaluate but it is, nevertheless, of central importance. Don't assume that at this point we are talking about music which is necessarily difficult or complex. In fact, it is most difficult to write music or words simply and at the same time beautifully. Perhaps that is the reason why there are so few hymn tunes written by "great" composers. The tune St. Anne ("O God, Our Help In Ages Past") is a good example of one which follows the rules and also has a quality of imagination which makes it feel "good". To sum this up, there truly is such a thing as good music.

In the church, however, other factors must be taken into account. Good music may not be good church music. First, one must consider objectives of the music. These should be compatible with the objectives of the Church at worship. They can be identified as

(1) the worship of God;

(2) self-examination and commitment;

(3) the nurturing of the community;

(4) the witness to the world;

Furthermore, Christian values do not lie in music itself but rather in the attitudes which attend its creation and hearing.

Concerning musicians' attitudes, Erik Routley, describes a situation wherein a "rustic" choir in England presents Beethoven's "Fidelio".[4] The professional competence of their singing was less than one would encounter in hearing the same production at the

Covent Gardens theater. Nevertheless, in its own way, it was an equally moving experience. The singers had done their homework. They had engaged in the disciplines of musical production to the absolute extremity of their capabilities. In performance, their commitment to the ideas being expressed had resulted in music which seemed to transcend their vocal limitations. This total commitment and involvement was apparent to the listeners. It provided a moving experience different from, though equal to that offered by more professional musicians. This, a matter of attitude, resulted in a very special kind of "goodness".

Another aspect of musical quality has to do with the way in which music is used. This consideration goes beyond its intrinsic musical value. To illustrate this, let us use the example of a hymn. Its tune can be evaluated by the musical criteria mentioned above - those of craftsmanship and inspiration or imagination.

Similarly, the text can be assessed by accepted standards as they operate within the disciplines of poetic writing. Furthermore, one can weigh the theological integrity of that text in the light of the beliefs of a particularly worshiping community. All of these are somewhat objective criteria, but altogether they are not enough. Routley has suggested that one can only judge a hymn to be "good" when it is "well written, well chosen, and well sung".[5]

We have just considered the "well-written" aspect involving matters of musical and poetic craftsmanship and theological understanding. The "well chosen" element connects directly with the four objectives of worship, self-examination, fellowship and witness.

It is not enough to choose a hymn just because it is loud or soft, familiar or unfamiliar. These matters are certainly important. However, other considerations are involved. The appropriateness of the text (should anyone give attention to it); the theological statements which are made or not made; the affirmation of personal faith which is assumed; the invitation to personal commitment which is invited. These are not just abstractions. They must be related to the specific context in which the hymn is to be used. If worship leaders ignore these considerations simply because they like the tune, they invite perfunctory or meaningless participation on the part of the congregation.

Further, even though the song in question has been well written and well chosen, it is not yet a good hymn until it has been well sung. Many things can inhibit this. Unfamiliarity, dead acoustics, lack of motivation on the part of the congregation, inept accompaniment, and many other factors can result in a hymn being sung poorly.

If a tree falls in the forest and no one is there to hear, is there any sound? The answer lies, of course, in the way the term "sound" is defined - whether it is vibration in the air or response to that vibration by the ear. Similarly, is "hymn" to be defined as a textual, musical, and theological statement or as a singing experience? In congregational worship, the hymn text and music is intended to serve and make possible a communal singing experience. If the congregation does not sing, the hymn fails to function as it was intended to. It cannot, then, be called a "good" hymn.

A pastor may choose a difficult, unfamiliar, unsingable hymn simply because the theological idea expressed fits the theme of the day. Was this, then, a good hymn? Not if one considers "good hymn" to be one which is well-sung - a fruitful congregational singing experience. We must remember that singing is not primarily a cognitive activity. It is a vocal one.

The importance of this was addressed by the 20th century theologian and pastor, Karl Barth. He was writing about the difficulty of expressing the Incarnation, God becoming human, in words which could really make sense. In his words:

How fortunate that when we are disturbed and oppressed by the problem of words we can flee to the realm of music, to Christian music and to a musical Christianity. Exactly because of its lack of concepts, music is the true and legitimate bearer of the message of Christmas.[6]

Speaking more generally about the primary importance of the singing experience, Barth said:

The community which does not sing is not the community...where it does not really sing but sighs and mutters spasmodically, shamefacedly, and with an ill grace, it can be at best only a troubled community which is not sure of its cause, and of whose ministry and witness there can be no great expectation... The praise of God which finds its concrete culmination in the singing of the community is one of the indispensable basic forms of the ministry of the community.[7]

Nothing here about the quality of the music or poetry. Nothing about the theological purity of the text. Only the simple suggestion that the Congregation must sing. It is commendable if that singing can utilize "good" music, poetry and theology. However, first there must be singing.

P.P. Bliss, author/composer of such songs as "Man of Sorrows", "Wonderful Words of Life" and many other 19th century gospel songs suggested:

No where is hypocrisy so woefully apparent, so generally tolerated, and so powerfully taught as in singing. What else can we expect when children see the church members turning leaves or idly gazing about the room while singing "Nearer My God to Thee".[8]

Truly, a "good" hymn must be well-sung "with the Spirit and with understanding". Since a hymn exists primarily as a vehicle for congregational expression, the degree to which this expression takes place is an essential part of its "goodness".

Finally, attitudes present in the whole process are relevant. Does the music appear to have been written in a manner which uses cliches which would be popular - which would sell? Was it chosen out of laziness or with the desire to show off one's musical or theological or hymnological expertise (pride)? Did it have the objective of manipulating people into a particular response? Was a hymn sung poorly because of the laziness of the congregation; sung well simply because it was an old favorite and the congregation refuses to sing anything but old favorites? Such attitudes deserve rebuke. All of the above considerations relating to attitude are appropriate to be considered before anyone can say with meaning "That was a good hymn".

In Routley's definition of a good hymn, quoted above, note that the first consideration, that of being "well written" is only one third of the criteria. In the last book that he wrote, 29 years later, Routley said that it is "...ten times more important that the hymn be chosen with sensitivity and understanding; a hundred times more important that it not be used to force people into accepting some value system desired by the leader".[9]

Consider another aspect of this issue. Many simplistic and unexamined attitudes about "good" church music find their way into the church community, by way of authority figures - musicians, pastors, teachers. These opinions may be very superficial, uninformed, or provisional and yet may persist and may shape one's understanding of value. Acceptance of such teaching may result in rigid opinions such as "The Gospel Songs of the late 19th century revival movement (e.g. "Near the Cross", "Blessed Assurance") are poor music, poetry, and theology". Or, "A good hymn must always be an expression of praise to God". One must be very careful about making or uncritically accepting such dogmatic statements. In the territory of "good" and "bad" in church music, such certainty is of questionable value.

Among those whose life and ministry is focused on the music and worship of the church, one often sees an enlarging of understanding, a shifting of priorities. The possibility itself of such enlarging and shifting should be an intentional part of our ministries and teaching. Therefore, some of the views of an "authority" will be changing rather than static.

In my own case, as a retired seminary professor, I am embarrassed by the remembrance of some of my own dogmatic teaching of several decades ago. Change has taken place in my understanding. Yet, from time to time I am reminded that some of these early pronouncements persist like ripples on a pond. Students have remembered and passed on teachings which I feel today were dreadfully misguided. Things change - see Chapter 2. We must be willing to question ideas that we once received as authoritative.

There is another problem with basing one's musical judgments on the perceived teaching of some authority figure. As a teacher, I know that it matters little what I think I said in any situation. Much more important is what the student thought he or she heard. A foundational "truth" held with great devotion may have been perceived erroneously from the beginning.

Do not let the issue of "goodness" in church music be settled with simplistic answers, nor let it be given permanent resolution. Situations and people change. Continued study and reflection and prayer are needed to deal with this.

Over the entrance to the music building in a Christian college is carved the phrase "Only the best is fit for the glory of God". This is a good statement. However, its real meaning may be quite different from that which the thoughtless and superficial reader assumes. Dare to engage in the constant search for that which is truly "best" in church music.

THE OLD WAYS
ARE MORE COMFORTABLE

Now we have a rationale which may be perfectly valid. The importance of this should not be overlooked. A significant aspect of our faith is that it offers comfort and reassurance. We all need this, and it is through the word of scripture, familiar liturgies, and the testimony of the Church through its hymns that God offers such comfort. It frequently comes through the medium of that which is familiar.

One need only examine the large quantity of hymns which emerged from Germany in the 17th century, written during the 30 Years War. Here are words of comfort and assurance and trust in God. (These are discussed at length in Chapter 7).

Of course, an important function of the Church is to offer comfort such as is expressed in these hymns.. The problem is not in the affirmation of this aspect of faith. Rather, it emerges when this becomes the whole message.

The prophet Amos warned of the dangers of complacency and godlessness when he said "Woe unto those who are at ease in Zion, and to those who feel secure on the mountain of Samaria". [Amos 6:1]. To expect only the comfortable in life and church is to refuse to receive the continual shedding of God's light and judgment upon our changing lives.

Roger Hazelton could have been speaking of music when he wrote about Christian art, saying:

> When the treatment is such as to banish or ignore all mystery or to gloss over the human doubt and anxiety which are so much a part of all religious searching, then the verities and profundities of genuine faith are distorted or degraded in favor of popular stereotypes and bland formulas.[10]

Remember Routley's comment quoted in the first chapter, "You weren't supposed to *like* that music". Occasionally the purpose of church music (and anything else in worship for that matter) is not to comfort but rather to press for your attention. It may be inviting you to consider some aspect of the faith which, though not comfortable, is part of the whole counsel of God.

Much of the Electronic Gospel offered by the T.V. church focuses on that which reassures and inspires. It frequently suggests or implies that God means nothing but good and prosperity for us all. That message alone is less than adequate. God can work in all things for good. However, we must remember the message of Job as we read that those who love God can experience tragedy and defeat. In the midst of Job's suffering he says "...I know that my redeemer lives, and at last he will stand on the earth". [Job 19:25] This becomes affirmation in the midst of very real adversity; adversity which may come at any time for any of us. This was the witness of the faith of the Church during the 30 Years War. The suffering and frustration was real, but faith in God can lead us into a higher reality.

The rough edges and sharp corners of reality, although not always comfortable, need to be experienced in worship - perhaps in some of the music.

FEAR OF
THE "DIFFERENT"

This heading is couched in a different form from those which precede it. It identifies something which is common to most of us, but which we are reluctant to identify or recognize. It is simply part of the human condition to fear that which is unfamiliar. If you feel that the word "fear" is too strong then substitute "be uncomfortable with". A catalog of possibilities would include: those whose race or culture is different from ours; those of greater or lesser wealth; those of greater or lesser education; those whose language is different - who speak English with difficulty ; those of different religion; those who are much larger or smaller in size; those who are handicapped. We are most at ease with persons who are just like us. The possibility for this same negative response exists in the field of music.

In summary, it is to be expected that each of us will have feelings of like or dislike about the music we encounter in church. To have such is neither unusual nor improper. However, I have attempted to suggest that often these are simply feelings, not well thought out, studied positions. I invite you to identify your feelings; to go further and try to discover upon what they are based. Identification and examination, of such personal foundational assumptions may help in entering into the uncomfortable but valuable process of change.

CHAPTER FOUR

An Interlude

At this point there is need for comment about that which is to follow - therefore, an "Interlude".

We have just been considering four arguments which are often used as rationale for supporting one's dislike of some church music. Others certainly exist, but these four are enough to illustrate the way in which preferences and prejudices may be formed and defended. Now we shall look at three specific types of music which are appropriate for today's church and see how such arguments might be used to support or reject them.

In the following chapters, three musical idioms have been used as examples:

Chapter 5. "POP" MUSIC AS USED BY THE CHURCH.

Sometimes such expression has been felt to be too "secular", inappropriate, or noisy and thus unsuited for Christian worship. At the present, however, pop-related church music is commonplace. In some situations it has even replaced most other traditional idioms.

Historically, there has been a recurring attempt on the part of the Church to use contemporary, colloquial, "pop" music in its worship, witness, and fellowship. We will examine the history of this process and related dynamics which have been present in the past 25 years.

Chapter 6. HYMNS WHICH ARE COMING TODAY FROM THE NON-WESTERN CHRISTIAN COMMUNITY (Asia, Africa, etc.). These may have images and tunes which are sometimes felt to be too strange for our worship.

The creation, awareness and use of such hymns is just beginning to take place. This is the first time in Christian history that there have been significant contributions of hymnological materials from the Third World. Should we use them? What about their strange sounds and language? Why are they important?

Chapter 7. CLASSIC HYMNODY AND CHURCH MUSIC. These musical expressions are sometimes felt to be dull, too historical, without excitement or contemporary relevance.

As far as attitudes are concerned, the "new" need not be something which bears today's date. I have used this term to refer to anything which is unfamiliar. Thus. hymns from two centuries ago may be "new" and, as such, uncomfortable for one who has recently entered the church as an adult and has no previous experience with such music. Nevertheless, classic hymnody may speak to our contemporary situation. For example, remember the mention of hymns from the 30 Year's

War. War is not only an historical issue. It is a vital part of our present concerns. It is upon this basis that we consider Classic Hymnody as something "new" and relevant.

Each of the above three types of music will be considered in the light of the four categories previously discussed:

(1) Is it biblical?

(2) Is it in our tradition?

(3) Is it good music?

(4) Is it comfortable?

Chapter 8 will focus on the process of bringing about change in the church. Chapter 9 deals with the scriptural concept of "Church". An understanding of the nature of this community must be the ultimate determinant of the music we use and of the ways in which we use it.

CHAPTER FIVE

"Pop" Music and the Church

In the past twenty years, various kinds of "pop" music have found a place in the worship of many churches. The point in addressing this matter is that while for many, this has been a cause for excitement and rejoicing, for others, it has been deeply troubling. Thus, it provides an excellent example of a specific musical idiom used in church about which some say, "I don't like that sound", or, "Even if I like it, it doesn't belong in church".

I have addressed this matter in my previous book, *Ministry and Music*[1] and will not to repeat the entire history of this movement. It is sufficient to say that for generations "pop" music has been a symbol of cultural evil. Enjoy the following historical catalog of comments concerning various pop music idioms. Many of these are from Nicholas Slonimsky's Lexicon of Musical Invective;[2]

1805 - THE WALTZ

From London:

Waltz is a riotous German Dance of modern invention. Having seen it performed by a select party of foreigners, we could not help reflecting how uneasy an English mother would be to see her daughter so familiarly treated, and still more to witness the obliging manner in which the freedom is returned by the females.

1899 - RAGTIME

A wave of vulgar, filthy and suggestive music has inundated the land. Nothing but ragtime prevails, and the cakewalk with its obscene posturings, its lewd gestures...It is artistically and morally depressing, and should be suppressed by press and pulpit.

1914 - THE TANGO

We condemn the dance of foreign origin known as the Tango, which by its lascivious nature offends morality. Christians ought not in conscience to take part in it. (Archbishop of Paris)

Said Cardinal O'Conner of Boston:

> If this Tango-dancing female is the new woman, then God spare us from any further development of the abnormal creature.

The Ambassador of Argentina to Paris stated formally:

> [The tango is] ...a dance peculiar to the houses of ill fame in Buenos Aires and is never cultivated in respectable gatherings.

1922-1934 - JAZZ

Comments by a pastor, Dr. A.W. Beaven in Rochester in 1922:

> Jazz may be analyzed as a combination of nervousness, lawlessness, primitive and savage animalism and lasciviousness.

In 1924 coach Knox of Harvard averred:

> Jazz parties give boys spindle legs and hollow chests.

The editor of Etude commented in 1925:

> We know that in its sinister aspects, jazz is doing a vast amount of harm to young minds and bodies not yet developed to resist evil temptations.

In 1934, Monsigneur Confrey of New York said:

> Jazz was borrowed from Central Africa by a gang of wealthy international Bolshevists from America, their aim being to strike at Christian civilization throughout the world.

1938 - SWING

Archbishop Frances Beckman told the National Council of Catholic Women in Biloxi, MI.:

> A degenerating and demoralizing musical system is given a disgusting christening as "swing" and turned loose to gnaw away at the moral fiber of young people...Jam sessions, jitterbugs, and cannibalistic rhythmic orgies are wooing our youth along the primrose path to hell.

The purpose of the above listing of criticisms of various forms of popular music is to show that every generation has problems with current "pop" music. Such concern has often been valid. "Pop" music does tend to emerge as rebellion against society's status quo. However, inevitably, such music soon finds broader acceptance and loses some of its negative connotations. In its most radical emerging forms it may have only very specialized occasional use in the church. However, some kinds of "pop" have always proved to be useful to the Christian community. In many situations they have become its most popular and characteristic musical expression.

A listing of objections raised in the 1980s concerning the rapidly-emerging use of "pop" music by the church might include the following:

1. It is a secular rather than sacred musical expression;
2. It has some kind of compulsive power over people;
3. It's too loud;
4. One can't understand the words;
5. It is associated with drugs, casual sex and, other unsavory aspects of contemporary life and thus certainly doesn't belong in church;
6. It's not good music.
7. I just don't like that kind of music.

Let us consider the above objections.

"IT'S SECULAR, NOT SACRED MUSIC"

What makes one kind of music "secular" while another is considered "sacred"? We have already considered the fact that the Bible does not make such explicit distinctions. In fact, the Bible simply does not discuss specific musical styles. It does not identify any music as "secular" or "sacred".

The use of instruments other than piano and organ in worship has frequently been related to this idea of "secular". When the New Testament speaks about music, it refers to the singing of all the people of God. Choirs are mentioned only in Revelation. There also one can find mention of instruments (trumpets) used as signals. In similar fashion, there are several passages in other New Testament writings which mention instruments, but none of these are a discussion about the use of music in worship. They are just part of the narrative or used to suggest a symbolic moment. Such might be, for instance, the announcement of the Lord's return and the judgment to follow.[3] The normative New Testament music is the singing of all of the Redeemed. Their singing is affirmed as part of the life of the community on earth and of the activity in heaven. Other than this, the New Testament makes no comment about the use of instruments in worship.

The use of instruments of many kinds is, of course, frequently mentioned in the Old Testament.[4] There also we find records of the structure and use of choirs.[5] However, for Christian worship, the New Testament material must be given priority. Older practices are relevant but must be must be considered in the light of the worship of the Community of the New Covenant.

If the New Testament is to be determinative, all musical instruments are equally suspect - organ and piano just as much as drums and guitar. This was exactly the position of John Calvin in the 1500s. Thus all instruments were forbidden by the 17th and 18th century Scottish Presbyterians, early Baptists in America, and other denominations which followed his teaching – some of them until the 20th century.

Since there is no explicit New Testament guidance to help us, the argument concerning "sacred" and "secular" music must be grounded on some foundation other than intrinsic nature or the use of "secular" instruments.

" POP MUSIC IS COMPULSIVE"

We have not yet attempted to define the term "pop music". I am using this to refer to anything which is included in today's commercial entertainment music. This may include rock, heavy metal, country western, jazz in any form, swing, ballads, show tunes, etc., etc. We must not generalize as if all of this body of music has the same characteristics,

Truly, some of these expressions have compulsive beat or seductive melodies and harmonies – characteristics which bring into question their appropriateness for worship. Much of "pop" music seeks response as its primary objective. However, this quality alone should not be used as an argument for either rejecting or affirming all of it. Let's be consistent. Some familiar compositions accepted as classical church music (Bach's "Preludes and Fugues", some choruses from Handel's "Messiah") demonstrate this quality. At least, one should evaluate all music by the same criteria before making a general condemnation.

The power of music is a relevant matter of concern. Ethnomusicology tells us that compulsive music is at the heart of much non-Christian worship. This is in contrast to the Christian faith in which God invites free, not contrived response. In the New Testament, Paul says concerning everything (including music) " 'All things are lawful for me', but I will not be enslaved by anything." [1 Cor. 6:12]

Where, then, does one draw the line? With Ravel's "Bolero"? With a Bach Toccata and Fugue? With Tschaikowsky's 5th Symphony? With many repetitions of an invitation hymn? With "pop" music that has a pronounced beat? This compulsive element in music is not restricted to any particular idiom, nor is it absent from traditional church music. Nevertheless, it should be recognized. Its intentional use for the purpose of compelling a desired response must be renounced.

The power of music is mentioned in 1 Samuel 10:5-11, also in 1 Samuel 18:10,11 where David is playing music to calm Saul. There are no comparable New Testament passages.

"IT'S
TOO LOUD!"

Often very true. However, this is a matter of personal preference, not at all confined to "pop" music.

In a recent worship service my wife and I were moved by the organ prelude which built up and up in volume until it reached a thrilling climax. Our guests in that service said, "That was too loud. It was painful and if it's typical of the music in this church we won't come again". The music which was exciting for one person was disturbing for another. Such differences of taste must be recognized and an attempt made to reconcile them with love and consideration. It is too simplistic to say simply "That was too loud" and assume that such a judgment settles the issue for everyone.

Another realistic problem may exist with those who are hard of hearing and who wear hearing aids. For them, any loud noise, whether speech or music, may be uncomfortable. Their concerns must be acknowledged. They should not determine the content of all worship music.

We have described above a difference of expectations and taste. These matters will be considered at length in the chapter "Agree To Disagree" Different preferences were operating. There is simply no way to say that some were right, others wrong. Different people simply liked different musical experiences.

Certainly, some "pop" music depends on sheer painful volume. The use of such in church would minister to a limited number of persons. However, we need to remember that all "pop" music is not loud, and all loud music is not "pop". Loudness in music must be dealt with apart from any particularly musical idiom.

"I CAN'T UNDERSTAND
THE WORDS"

Again, this may be very true. However, as above, let us put this criticism into perspective. Unfortunately, this statement is true not only of "pop" music - it is also characteristic of many choir anthems or solos.

Perhaps the soloist or choir has never learned to phonate consonants and to clearly articulate words and phrases. The individual or choir may be more concerned with producing a beautiful tone than with clearly expressing words. In such a case, the text being sung will probably be unintelligible.

Furthermore, some choir music, including some of the great "classics" may have various sections of the choir singing different words at the same time. For example, consider some of the choruses of Handel's "Messiah". In these the musical priorities have overtaken the textual ones. The listener is invited to the theme, for example "Hallelujah". The words become vehicles to carry the music along in expressing this motif. It isn't of central importance that they be understandable.

The text is presumed to be important in most choir or solo music. Nevertheless, some music is not always constructed so as to make communication of that text possible. This is also true in much "pop" music.

The answer in any case - print the words in the order of service. Don't depend on the skill or priorities of the singers. Such procedure has the further advantage of providing something for the worshiper to reflect on and to anticipate.

The over-arching principle in each of the above sections is the same. Be critical - but use the same criteria to evaluate all music, not just that which you dislike.

"IT HAS UNCHRISTIAN ASSOCIATIONS"

This is a matter of valid concern. Certainly some pop music speaks implicitly or explicitly about drugs, casual sex, witchcraft or other unsavory aspects of life. We have already suggested that pop music has always been a symbol of cultural evil. The tango, Ragtime, Jazz, Swing, Rock, mentioned above have all been condemned because of their associations with the contemporary rebellion within society. However, since the 1960s, some "pop" music idioms have been used by young Christians to express their faith in contemporary musical terms. Dare we say that such expression must always be considered to be inappropriate?

We find ourselves in the territory of associations. What the Church often fails to realize is that associations can be changed. There is nothing to prevent the linking of new Christian words and ideas with a tune or an idiom that was previously a very secular expression. This has happened many times in the past. Remember "O Sacred Head Now Wounded".

Are you familiar with J. Edwin Orr's hymn text "Search Me O God"? This hymn was written in the early 1940s and was set to a traditional Maori tune? At about the same time, the top tune on the "Lucky Strike Hit Parade" was the love song "Now Is The Hour" which used the same music. In a Christian conference setting Orr was asked "Doesn't it bother you to think of this song being used in church when people may be thinking of the secular words?" His response, "No. Rather, it delights me to think of this being used at a U.S.O. (service men's) dance with hearers thinking of the words 'Search Me O God'" Associations can be changed.

In such a case, the playing or hearing of such a tune outside of the church can be a stimulus to Christian affirmation. It can serve to recall the "sacred" rather than the "secular" associations. We are not confined to the meanings that the non- Christian world gives to music. "Heavy Metal" sound will not speak of Christ to those of us who have nothing but other associations with this music. However, it is possible that the Christian young person who is part of a "Heavy Metal" group can use this sound to express the present reality of Jesus Christ for himself or herself?

The church has two options concerning this matter of musical association. It can simply reject all "secular" expressions. This is the safe way to go. However, following this course has the result, for many people, of eliminating from worship anything in music that speaks of the contemporaneity of Jesus Christ.

That raises the question of how we are going to connect the worship experience of the Church with the present world in which the congregation moves daily. Such connection involves the theological question as to whether worship is to be a retreat from the world, "a place of quiet rest, near to the heart of God", or whether it should have real relationships with everyday life. If the latter, then how do we make such connectives? One of the potential values of "pop" music is its ability to impersonate the "world" in the midst of our worship.

It is appropriate for the Church to build bridges between its worship and everyday life outside of the sanctuary. This can be done in its music as well as in other ways. If we attempt this, several factors will be relevant:

1. We need not use the most extreme forms of "pop" music as we bring some of this expression into worship.

2. A quite different concern is that we should be aware of whether music which we include for this purpose is truly "pop". The church now has a great deal of sanitized "Christian pop" which is the colloquial musical expression of a generation ago, "Oldies but goodies" This idiom can be pleasant and safe for those who belong to that generation; it may have little to do with the musical expression of today.

3. Related to the last point, history demonstrates the fact that across the centuries, the Church has, from time to time, included popular musical expressions. These have then been conserved. In time, their meaning has changed until, by association, they have come to represent traditional church music. The associations related to "pop" music are transient. They can and will be changed, whatever we do.

"THIS MUSIC
IS NOT GOOD MUSIC"

This is true - sometimes, but not always. Much popular music is nothing but junk. So is a great deal of contemporary Christian music which is produced primarily for its commercial value.

Part of the problem for many of us is that we react against a musical stereotype without having any personal experience with the music itself. In the mid 1960s my teen-aged daughters, knowing my strong reaction against the music of the Beetles, said one day "Dad, sit down and be quiet and listen". I did that, and, assisted by a sabbatical year in Scotland, discovered that I liked the Beetles. What's more, some of their music belonged in my category of "good music". I had just never taken time to listen to them. I didn't like their long hair.

It was a gratifying reinforcement that subsequently, Leonard Bernstein, conductor of the New York Philharmonic Orchestra, presented a T.V. program in which he said and demonstrated that "The Beatles are the most creative and innovative force in the field of music today".

About the same time, the respected New York music critic, Henry Pleasants, in the book The Agony of Modern Music, said about jazz:

> Thus the jazz accomplishment is simply defined. It has taken music away from the composers and given it back to the musicians and their public...[The contemporary composer is]...a pathetic figure seeking to shape the music of his generation while all around him the music of his generation is spontaneously and irresistibly taking place.[6]

To say that music is "pop" music does not necessarily mean that it is all bad music.

Another matter - the Church has a history of using, losing and regaining the concept of "disposable music". Some of this will be pop-related. There is no basis for feeling that all music of the church must be great music. "Praise Choruses", very popular today, cannot be affirmed in general by musical criteria. However, they serve a purpose which is valuable in today's church. We must remember this concept of "disposable music" - music which serves a purpose for the moment and then is discarded or re-placed by something more contemporary.

The great hymn writer, Charles Wesley wrote more than 6500 hymn texts - yet only 50 are retained in the current Methodist hymn book, that of the denomination which he and his brother started. Most of the rest of them were "disposable". They fitted a particular time and place in the life of the church. They are not relevant for today. They were not great poetry or music. The passage of time, however, sorts these out and will bring about affirmation of a few and discarding of the rest. "Disposability" in music only becomes a problem when we seek to canonize such expressions and try to equate them with the great classic hymns of the Church. Thus we must try to discriminate between the transient and the timeless expressions of faith. Each has its own appropriate place in worship.

This same process of discrimination needs to take place continually with any familiar things which we use from a generation or two ago. This is certainly true concerning "church pop" of 25 years ago. It also applies with church music in the more "classical" idiom.

> "In the tension between the contemporary and the traditional we should make distinction between our rich heritage of sacred art and music, and tradition in the sense of perpetuating the bad habits of the past. We seldom understand the genius of the age just ahead of us and tend to perpetuate the worst our grandfathers did, especially in the arts. A later age discovers their best characteristics."[7]

"I DON'T LIKE
SUCH MUSIC"

There can be no argument with this. Do remember, however, that all new experiences will tend to need nurturing. This is true when encountering new food, new persons, new worship, or new music.

Be reminded of our focus in this book. We are dealing primarily with the music of the Sunday morning worship service. Hopefully, there will be other gatherings using a variety of music styles. If the music used in these disturbs you but seems fitting for the group, just don't attend. Sunday Worship, however, should be the one occasion that brings together the whole congregation in all of its wonderful variety.

In any case, you can be sure that there will be other people who don't like some of your favorites. We shall address this issue in the final chapter "Agree to Disagree" The point of *this* chapter is to suggest that this issue has always been with the church. New music comes as "pop". It is used by some and rejected by others. In its use it is tempered or gentled, and it becomes the carrier of associated Christian values and experiences. In a relatively short time this idiom as used by the Church becomes itself a kind of "church music" - it is no longer offensive.

By the time this book comes into print there will probably be some new kind of "pop". The Church will then need to deal with it. Somewhere there will be an attempt to use it to express the contemporaneity and "worldliness" of the Gospel. Critical but patient consideration will again be needed. Be assured that God will continue to use "that which is old and that which is new".

CHAPTER SIX

Church Music from the Non-Western World

Something remarkable is happening today in God's Church. For the first time in Christian history, in the non-Western world, original hymns are being written and set to indigenous music. Occasionally these are being translated into English for use in our Western English-speaking culture. A brief historical review may help one to be able to better appreciate what is happening at this moment.

THE CHURCH'S MUSICAL TRADITION

For centuries, missionaries have gone from the West (Europe, Great Britain, America) to countries in the South and East, carrying the Gospel of Jesus Christ. They took with them two books - the Bible and a hymn book or psalter. As soon as possible, they translated portions of scripture into the local language. Eventually, they had Christian converts and a worshipping community. However, because of the very nature of this process, that community had no Christian songs of its own. The obvious and customary solution to this problem was for the missionary to translate Western hymns, using their tunes from Western culture, and to teach them to the new Christians.

This process as well as the next steps which I will identify took place all over the world, though not always at the same chronological time. It still takes place in the late 20th century. The sequence was always the same. Translations of hymns from the West became the common expression of Christian communities around the world.

Such a procedure was, originally, a very logical and innocent one. However, before long, this music from the West became the *only* acceptable Christian music. It symbolized the new life in Christ and the new community which was His Church. After all, the drums and flutes and other indigenous musical instruments and musical styles were part of the old non-Christian life. Such expressions of "pagan culture" should have no place in this new worship. This was the common attitude. Such music was condemned for Christian use - as were many other parts of the old culture.

In my library of hymnals from around the world, one can find the hymn "O God, Our Help in Ages Past" translated into Kikongo,

Bulu, Tamil, Naga, Hawaiian, Japanese, Chinese, Korean, and, perhaps 100 other languages. "When I Survey the Wondrous Cross" appears in Samoan, Thai, Indonesian, Kachin, Vietnamese, Eskimo, Navajo, Hopi, many languages and dialects from the Philippines, the Cook Islands, Papua New Guinea. The point is that both of these hymns originated in England, early in the 1700s. They were written by Isaac Watts, set to British or American tunes, and imported to the world. It is not unusual to find a hymn book in one of the above languages without a single original indigenous text or tune. Even today such collections of Western hymns in Eastern languages are still being printed. There are occasional exceptions to this general practice. For instance, in 1853 a collection of Tamil "Christian Lyrics", indigenous texts and tunes, was printed in India. However, such acceptance of national expression was uncommon.

CHANGES
IN ATTITUDE

Around the beginning of the 20th century, some enlightened missionaries began to reconsider this practice of totally rejecting anything of indigenous culture. They asked questions such as, "Can faith in Jesus Christ and worship of Him be expressed only in Western terms?" and " Why cannot the everyday things which are a part of some local culture be consecrated to Christ, given new meanings, and used to live out commitment to the True God?" However, such questioning was remarkable, not typical.

By mid-century, another factor emerged. After World War Two, there was a great rise of nationalism. Many Third World countries began to affirm their traditions as never before. National musical roots were perceived as having value. The study and use of them was nurtured.

As some missionaries tried to reconsider the traditional practices, an interesting and unexpected phenomenon emerged. Resistance was met from many national Christians who had learned well the lesson that their own music was truly "pagan" - unfit for Christian use. Other nationals felt the need for such a change but their suggestions were rejected by the community. A young man came from Nagaland to study music at a seminary in Berkeley. His first question, and the desire that had motivated him to come was this, "How can I get my people to be willing to use their own music in worship? They resist anything that is not from the West." He was not alone in this concern. At a class for pastors in Papua New Guinea, one young but experienced Melanesian minister shared his experience. "We built a new (thatch) church in our village. On the day when we dedicated it, we had the members of the community bring all their musical instruments. As part of the consecration service, we dedicated these instruments to the service of Christ." Here was an intelligent and sensitive procedure to deal with the problem.

Today there is a growing desire on the part of Christians of many cultures around the world to make use of their own music. While teaching in India, I tutored an Assamese seminary music teacher whose objective was to become more skilled in notating music. His desire was to be able to take folk tunes from Northeast India, write them down, and use them to accompany Christian words. His concerns are shared by many others.

At the same time It is most exciting that in the West we are beginning to discover such music; to translate these texts into English; to use these tunes; even to encourage publication of them. Thus, for the first time in Christian history, the Church of the West is beginning to have at hand hymns written by Christian brothers and sisters in non-Western cultures. Several major denominational hymnals published in the last few years have included a significant number of non-Western hymns and tunes.[1]

THE CONTEMPORARY SITUATION

The present context in which these indigenous expressions are appearing should be considered. Their emergence is related to the growth and maturing of the Church in the Non-Western world. Using the World Christian Encyclopedia.[2] As a source for late 20th century statistics, consider the following:

- In 1900 two-thirds of all the Christians in the world were in Europe and Russia; by the year 2,000, three-fifths of them will be living in Africa, Asia, and South America;

- The Western churches are losing practicing Christians at the rate of 7,000 each day; the church in Africa is adding 4,000 Christians each day through baptism;

- The largest growth in the Third World is not in those churches tied to traditional Western denominations but rather is in indigenous expressions of the Church.

We in the West have traditionally functioned as parent/teacher/leader to the Church in the rest of the world. The time is at hand when our children in Christ around the world are growing to be responsible adults; our pupils are becoming our peers; our followers are coming to the place where God may be trying to use them to be our leaders. National leaders overseas are saying "How can people who are seeing a decline in membership in their own churches help us in evangelism?".[3] The new hymnody which is emerging from this part of the world may help us to understand what is happening in these churches which are part of today's global village.

All of this seems to be a long way from the basic focus of this book. Let us examine the issue in the light of the questions we have been asking of each idiom.

IS IT SCRIPTURAL?

As with "pop" music, there is no explicit scriptural discussion of Western or Non-Western musical styles and idioms. Accepting this, we must go to expressions in the Bible which have implications for the question. These tend to be of two types - those which affirm the universality of the Church and those which suggest separation from the environment in which the Church finds itself.

Consider the Apostle Paul's frequently-quoted affirmation "There is neither Jew nor Greek, there is neither slave nor free, there is neither male nor female; for you are all one in Christ Jesus." [Gal. 3:28] This gives no priority to Western (or Jewish, or Indian) understandings and practices. It simply suggests that all of humanity is equal before Christ. It leaves the door open for God's Spirit to speak to His Church and to the world through any who are committed to Jesus Christ, no matter what their race and culture.

The issue of "separation" involves the concept that there are aspects of the "world" which are intrinsically unchristian and are thus to be avoided. There are a number of New Testament passages which say in one way or another "You are to be different from the world". Such passages have sometimes been viewed as referring to matters of clothing, jewelry, transportation, music, etc. In truth, they address the issues of values and objectives for the Christian life. They tell us to have other goals and methods, other priorities and values than those of the non-Christian world.

Denominations and congregations have formed and divided over this issue. Biblical scholars with much more expertise than mine have dealt with this subject. I dare to suggest that God is not trying to tell us whether to have musical instruments in church, wear or not wear jewelry, or dress in a certain way. God's concern, as addressed to us in Scripture, is rather that we put first the Kingdom of God. We are to have priorities in our lives which conform with our commitment to be Christ's Body in today's world. We are to establish and follow a Christian hierarchy of values. Christ's priorities were not with matters of food and drink, clothing, musical instruments - matters of religious law. They had to do with being God's loving, healing, reconciling presence in the world. "Do not conform yourselves to the standards of this world, but let God transform you inwardly by a complete change of your mind. Then you will be able to know the will of God - what is good and is pleasing to him and is perfect." [Rom. 12:2]

Remember the discussion earlier about making an idol of one's theological ideas. Perhaps some of the Church has been doing this about its music, thus excluding the possibility of "foreign" expressions. Scripture does not assign a higher value to music of the West than of the East, nor does it suggest that music from the rest of the world is less "Christian".

IS IT
TRADITIONAL?

Let's look at traditions. Today we assume that any hymnbook will probably include hymns from a number of differing theological and denominational sources. However, less than two hundred years ago, it was customary that Baptists would sing Watts (Calvinist); Methodists sang hymns by Wesley (Arminian); Lutherans and Brethren sang German chorales; Presbyterians and Reformed would sing only Psalms and other passages of scripture. Commonly, hymn books would contain a selection of hymns by one author or of one group of authors whose theological views were compatible with those using the collection.

The first truly ecumenical hymnal to be widely used was Hymns Ancient and Modern which was published in England in 1863. It became the model for an inclusive hymnal such as we take for granted today. Even that collection was without Gospel Songs which were arising about the same time in the United States. We assume that most contemporary books will include some of these as well as a variety of hymns without regard for the theology, place, or time of the authors. For us today, the theology expressed in the hymn text is important; that of the author is irrelevant. We are much more pragmatic and acceptant than in earlier times. We have already broken with the tradition of severely limiting the kinds of hymns we are willing to sing.

Two hundred years ago the inclusion of non-Western hymns, had they been available, would have been unthinkable. Today, such practice is perfectly in accord with our expectation that the hymn book should reflect the songs of the whole family of God. We are simply gaining a wider view of the extent of this family.

An example of the inclusion of hymns from a different minority culture, can be seen in the growing acceptance of the centuries- old Black Spiritual (for example, "Swing Low Sweet Chariot"). Many non-Black congregations and hymnal editors are including these songs today. Their great worth and usefulness as part of our Christian tradition is being recognized.[4]

This is something more than a change within the Church; it is also a change in society. "Black Gospel" has become an important idiom in today's entertainment music. Also, in the 20th century the Black Spiritual is finding a more important place in general culture. For more than a generation it has been common, even expected, that a school choir concert would include a group of spirituals. In similar fashion, today in the arena of secular music we are encountering music from the Third World. Our traditions are being reviewed and changed, both in society and in the Church.

Is the use of such "foreign" songs consistent with our early traditions? No! Neither is our present practice nor that of many generations past.

Certainly, in their history, many denominational congregations have experienced what it means to be part of a minority group within a dominant culture. However, the hymns which they have produced have not been as radically different as some of those non-Western ones which we are considering. Previously, texts and tunes, even if unfamiliar, made use of idioms which were common to the Church in the West. The next two questions deal with the more radical difference sometimes found in these Non-Western hymns.

IS IT
GOOD MUSIC?

Yes and no. At this point we must apply all the criteria that we might use to evaluate any other kinds of musical and textual expression. Some of the music is truly well written; some seems to be quite superficial. The tunes may be well written by Western standards. However, there are additional factors unique to this non-Western music that are relevant. Many of these songs were created in a culture whose music is radically different from ours. Sometimes distortion takes place in bringing an indigenous tune into Western notation. The problem is even greater when a tonal language (such as Chinese) is involved in the original.

The question posed at the beginning of this section assumes that we are thinking in terms of Western music. One might also ask whether the music, poetry, and theology is "good" in terms of the culture in which the hymn originated. To make this judgment, we must call upon non-Western ethnomusicologists or music historians. For example, a Christian musician in a non-Western culture may write a hymn tune that is nothing more than a poor imitation of one from the West - "good" in neither culture.

Some of the texts (which, by definition, exist for us only in translation) are skillfully and imaginatively translated. No generalization is possible. We must remember that a translation of any hymn text originating in a language other that English is a new creation. Thus we owe a great debt to John Wesley and Catherine Winkworth who have given us so many translations of German hymns. Similarly, we are indebted to John Mason Neale and other 19th century British translators who, as part of the Oxford Movement, brought ancient Greek and Latin hymns into beautiful English for our use.

Evaluations concerning poetry are difficult since we have lost the original writings in the process of translation. Some images are cross-cultural; others are not. As to theology, are we asking whether the theology expressed in the hymn is consonant with our theology? Such an assumption is an arrogant one. Rather, it is possible that God, the Holy Spirit, might be trying to enlarge our theological understanding through hymn-writing brothers and sisters in the non-Western world.

It is evident that matters of artistic value are more difficult to deal with in this situation. Perhaps now is the time to revisit Chapter 3 and to recall the suggestion that "goodness" in church music has many dimensions.

Dare to try some of these new songs. Let the critical, selective process wait for a bit until you are more at ease with the idiom. Some of the songs which are mentioned below might be good things with which to begin.

Finally we come to the question:

IS IT COMFORTABLE?

As always, anything new will be less comfortable than that which is familiar. In addition there are characteristics of some of these non-Western tunes which give them a unique aspect of strangeness.

Some are friendly and have a familiar feeling. They are easily sung. Examples might be "Father, Son and Spirit" with a gentle and harmonious Maiori tune.[5] Another, from the Philippines is the text "Father in Heaven" set to the tune of an old Philippine lullaby.[6] Both of these are easily learned.

Other tunes, which sound more characteristically Asian, are the settings for the texts "Golden Breaks the Dawn"[7] and "My heart Looks in Faith" from the Chinese.[8] The Japanese church has given us characteristic music for "Here O Lord Your Servants Gather".[9] These Asian hymns work best when sung in unison. They are essentially pentatonic (using only 5 notes as do many Black spirituals). The tunes, while singable, will provide a distinctive "foreign" musical sound. Their texts offer some refreshing new images. They are capable of introducing the world community to a local congregation.

Still another type of song offers delightful fun. From Africa, there is the "call and response" Swahili hymn "He Has Conquered Death".[10] This cannot be sung in traditional hymn fashion. Neither can it be expressed appropriately with restraint and care. It demands a wholehearted congregational responsive shout, with abandon - "He has done the Father's will completely; He has conquered death". Another song, one of the most widely used hymns from Africa is "Fill Us With Your Love".[11]

From the Caribbean, we are offered the calypso rhythm and simple expression of "Enter Into Jerusalem. Let Us Go To God's House".[12]

A survey of the use of such songs in recent hymnals is available in a recent issue of the journal of the Hymn Society.[13]

To introduce such songs involves running the risk of "I don't like that". The tunes and/or texts may be a bit strange. They will certainly be unfamiliar. Their intrusion into the life of the church may be unsettling. Perhaps this is precisely what we need. It may be that persons from the Third World are not physically present in our congregation. We still need to hear their voices; to share their affirmations of faith in God through Jesus Christ.

Such songs should not be presented as something strange and curious like interesting clothes and food from another culture. They represent Christian witness from the growing edge of the Church. Our response needs to be more than interest in the curious and novel. Rather, we are being invited to listen to and share that which the Spirit may be trying to say to us which can enlarge our Christian faith and understanding.

Christians of the non-Western world no longer require our approval. Rather, we need to share their insights and their witness to the vitality of Jesus Christ alive in their lives and cultures.

CHAPTER SEVEN

Traditional Hymnody as "The New"

The "new" can be defined as "anything beyond the present experience and appetites of a particular congregation". It need not mean only that which is contemporary. It can include old and traditional hymnody when that body of music is unfamiliar. However, before exploring this, it is important that we first consider the role of memory in the life of a congregation.

MEMORY
AND THE CHURCH

Memory is an essential ingredient in providing healthy self-understanding, both for an individual and for an organization. We cannot know who we are without knowing who we were and where we have been. Amnesia is simply the state in which an individual lacks this essential knowledge. Such a condition is unfortunate. A church as well as a person may lack this self-understanding - may have "amnesia". For a congregation to fail to have a corporate memory means that there is confusion as to what it should be and do. This memory includes the remembrances of the "old timers" and the anniversary celebrations of the church. However, that is only the beginning. It must reach backwards to the generations and centuries of Christian experience.

Much has been said concerning the fundamental role of memory in communal life. The 20th century Jewish philosopher, Abraham Heschel addressed this as he wrote "Only he who is an heir is qualified to be a pioneer."[1]

Upon entering the National Archives building in Washington, D.C. one can read these words: "The heritage of the past is the seed bed that brings forth the harvest of the future". The writer of Hebrews says (in a different context, but relevant for today) "Remember your leaders, those who spoke to you the word of God; consider the outcome of their life and imitate their faith".[Heb. 13:7] For us, these leaders must include the Wesleys and Roger Williams, Calvin and Luther, Wycliffe and Huss, St. Francis and Augustine, and all who have taught and tried to live out the word of God.

WHERE, IN THE CHURCH, IS SUCH MEMORY FOUND?

SCRIPTURE

From its beginning the Bible tells us about God's gathering and dealing with His people - "The People of God". In the New Testament we learn of the forming of the communities which will become the Christian Church. Then the biblical canon is closed. Scripture tells us nothing about what God has done in and through His Church from that time until now. Thus, a congregation may justly pride itself on knowing and following the Scriptures and yet be unaware of what God has continued to reveal and do across the centuries as He has guided His people.

CREEDS AND CONFESSIONS

Throughout history, theological understandings and commitments of the Church have been formulated and preserved in its creeds and confessions.

For the Liturgical Church, these are an ever-present part of worship. They thus provide a continuing memory of that which the Church has believed.

Within the Free Church[2], this is not always the case. Some denominations (for example, the Baptists) have traditionally resisted any use of creeds or any commitment to them. They have felt that God's revelation is to be found solely within the local congregation. Other church groups do not resist the creeds - they simply ignore them.

CLASSICAL LITURGIES

Within the Liturgical Church, orders of service are regularly used which are essentially from many centuries ago.[3] The use of these provides a common experience of worship which reaches back across many generations. One should be aware that for 1,000 years prior to the Reformation, most Christian worship was governed by some kind of officially approved liturgy. In the monastery, the town and the cathedral, some kind of service book was used which gave directions for the procedures and content of worship.

In the Free Church, the idea of worshiping through the use of such a set form contradicts its basic understanding of the nature of worship. Such worshipers feel that God's Spirit must be allowed freedom to move and direct. (Unfortunately, the worship of a Pentecostal or Baptist congregation may be as predictable and unvarying as that of an Episcopal one. It will just lack the historical dimension.)

CLASSICAL PRAYERS

"Almighty God, unto whom all hearts are open, all desires known, from whom no secrets are hid; cleanse the thoughts of our hearts by the inspiration of thy Holy Spirit that we may perfectly love thee and worthily magnify thy holy name; through Jesus Christ, our Lord."[4]

Today, this prayer for purity of heart is prayed, often weekly, by Methodist, Episcopalian, Anglican, Lutheran, Church of South India, and many other congregations. It was prayed by George Washington, by Shakespear, and by the first Queen Elizabeth. In her time it was already old and familiar, having come from the 13th century Latin liturgy of Sarum (Salisbury). There are many such prayers which are part of the Church's memory and are still in use today in the Liturgical Church.

As with creeds, the Free Church makes little or no use of such materials. With some pastors and parishioners they may simply be unknown. Others reject such "set" prayers as being a hindrance to the free working of the Spirit. Fortunately, a greater knowledge of these treasures and a more acceptant attitude concerning their use is emerging.

THEOLOGICAL AND DEVOTIONAL WRITINGS

Of course the Church's memory is to be found in such literature.

Concerning the theological writings, it is likely to be only the pastor who has encountered Augustine's *Confessions*, Luther's *Table Talks* or Calvin's *Institutes*. Even this encounter may be limited to a seminary experience somewhere in the past.

Laity may be more familiar with historical devotional materials such as a 'Kempis' Imitation of Christ, Brother Lawrence's *Practice of the Presence of God*, Kelly's *A Testament of Devotion*, Fenelon's *Christian Perfection*.

The reading of such classics can provide a link with the historical faith of the Church. It is not to be expected that familiarity with such writings will be normative. Most members of Sunday morning's congregation will neither know about nor read them.

CLASSIC HYMNODY
AS THE CHURCH'S MEMORY

It is in the hymn book that we find the most readily-available contact with our Christian roots. The hymnal contains texts which speak of the faith and experience of God's People across the centuries. This is true, even though they are frequently unrecognized as such testimony. Wesley's "O For A Thousand Tongues" may be sung simply as a song of praise. There may be no awareness of its origin, written by Charles Wesley to celebrate the first anniversary of his dramatic conversion to Jesus Christ.

Today, many churches exist on a musical diet consisting largely of materials created in the past two decades. Others may add gospel songs from late 19th century revivalism. Praise choruses abound - classic hymnody may be virtually unknown. In such a church, exceptions to this practice may be made at Christmas, Easter, and, occasionally, Thanksgiving. Somehow, at these high special times we tend to be a bit more receptive to some of the traditional songs of the Church.

Missing from this hymnological diet may be:

- the traditional American/English hymns from the 19th century;

- great hymns of Wesley and Watts which have survived from the 18th century;

- rich German hymnody - mainly from the 17th century.

This body of song includes both the affirmations of faith
from the 30 Year's War and the devotional expressions
of the German Pietistic movement;

- Reformation hymnody - the metrical Psalms and German Chorales which were a major dynamic force in the
Protestant Reformation;

- Ancient hymns of the Church from the early and middle
ages.

For such a church, to "sing a new song" might well mean to
discover or express new understandings of God through the singing of classic or ancient hymns. I suggest that such hymns may
provide some values necessary to nurture the full life of the congregation.

A STABILIZING INFLUENCE

A plan of the theological history of the church might show
something resembling the track of a meandering river. Wide swings
to right and left are visible. Loops develop that momentarily seem
of primary importance and then are cut off to remain as curious
backwaters. Others emerge and are built upon as major way-
stations.

Consider the "Death of God" thought of the 1960s. This received an enormous amount of public and ecclesiastical attention. It was embraced by some, misunderstood by many, and
seriously questioned in some informed circles. 25 years later, the
emotional responses and, in fact, widespread concern about the
issue has virtually vanished. Some valuable insights emerging
from this movement have contributed to the understandings of

the Church. Nevertheless, for most of today's worshipers it is unknown or irrelevant.

In the midst of this emotion-laden episode of the Church, the classic hymns were at hand. They could serve, if known and used, in the words of Karl Barth:

> ....to carry one through historicism and anti-historicism, mysticism and rationalism, orthodoxy, liberalism, and existentialism, [the "death of God"?] and to bring one back some day to the matter itself.[5]

In the classic hymns of the Church, one can find a distillate of Christian belief across the centuries. Miller Patrick has said;

> Every great quickening of the Church's life, every fierce conflict through which it has passed, every new momentum which it has received, has left its legacy of song for the enrichment of subsequent ages. A Book like this {The Church Hymnary] illustrates the unity of the Church, underlying all its differences.[6]

SHARED EXPERIENCE

HYMNS CAN BE INTER-GENERATIONAL

First, within the local congregation, classic hymns can provide common ground for worship experiences for the old and the young.. It is true that there are songs for children which are appropriate for them and inadequate or a bit embarrassing for adult expression ("Jesus Wants Me For A Sunbeam"). Equally, there are many adult hymns whose imagery, language, and theological concepts are inappropriate for children ("O Sacred Head Now Wounded").

Nevertheless, within classic hymnody there are many hymns which can be shared with children and adults. It is not necessary that the children comprehend everything expressed in a hymn. It is necessary that they understand something. Examples of hymns able to provide common ground might be "This Is My Father's World", "Jesus Loves Me", "The Lord's My Shepherd", "Fairest Lord Jesus".

The second aspect of this "inter-generational" characteristic has enormous dimensions. Through classic hymnody we are able to share the faith and experience of those from other generations across the centuries who have known Jesus Christ and found strength and purpose in Him.

Blind Fanny Crosby's more than 6,000 gospel songs, written over a century ago tell of her radiant faith which transcended physical infirmity ("To God Be The Glory", "All The Way My Savior Leads Me"). Wesley's equally numerous hymns of the 1700s speak of the reality of a personal relationship with Jesus Christ ("Jesus, Lover of My Soul", "O For A Thousand Tongues"). Watts' hymns, written early in that century, remind us of the sovereignty of God ("O God, Our Help in Ages Past"). The German hymns written during the 30 years war of the 1600s provide a unique body of testimony of the power of God to reveal Himself in a time of war. Here are words of comfort and assurance and trust in God. Yet this period of German History has been described by Williston Walker, the church historian, as a time when:

> The land had been ploughed from end to end for a generation by lawless and plundering armies. Population had fallen from sixteen million to less than six. Fields were

waste. Commerce and manufacturing destroyed...Little evidence of spiritual life was manifested in this frightful time of war.[7]

He continues, reminding us that the hymns of Paul Gerhardt emerged from the tragedy of those troubled times.

The Encyclopedia Britanica says of this period in history:

....Germany was the battleground for French, Spanish, Swedish, and Austrian armies which...reduced the country to a state of misery that no historian has been able to describe, save by detailing the horrors of one or another village among the thousands that were ruined.[8]

In spite of this, Christians of that time affirmed in their singing and worship a kind of reality which transcended the chaos and suffering and absurdity of their everyday experiences.[9]

Hymns of the 1500s include metrical Psalms from Calvin ("All People That On Earth Do Dwell") and Luther's confident "A Mighty Fortress Is Our God". These can remind us of the struggles for Church renewal that took place during the Protestant Reformation.

From medieval times we have many monastic songs of devotion ("O Sacred Head Now Wounded", "Jesus, Thy Boundless Love To Me"). From even earlier centuries come songs expressing doctrine and praise (Shepherd of Tender Youth", "All Glory, Laud and Honor").

All of these combine to tell us that God has continued to love and guide His people. Their situations may be not unlike ours today. God offers us wisdom and strength through the hymn book in a way second only to the scriptures themselves.

HYMNS CAN BE INTER-CONGREGATIONAL

Let me summarize what was said in the chapter on "pop" music. In the 1960s and 1970s there was an explosion of new music - Christian folk and "pop". This was an exciting time for church musicians. Throughout history, "sacred" and "secular" musical idioms have tended to have distinctive and differing characteristics and associations. In the 16th century, Luther and Calvin were accused of introducing "tavern tunes" and Geneva jigs". Two centuries later, the Wesleys included a style of tunes for some of their new hymns which resembled those found in John Gay's then-contemporary "Begger's Opera". In late 19th century America, the emerging "gospel hymn" included tunes which sounded like the popular parlor music of the day.

In each of the examples above, Christian texts were set to popular music. At the same time as they gained favor in the Church, the secular popular music of society developed new musical idioms. It is the nature of the Church to tend to conserve anything that it finds useful. Eventually, such music which began as an attempt to relate church music to popular taste became part of the distinctive repertoire of the Church and was heard nowhere else. (400 years ago, this process took several generations; today it happens in a few decades.)

In the 1960s there was a similar revolution in church music. A great outpouring of religious songs using popular music of the time (mainly in the folk idiom) began. Musicians in many local congregations were encouraged to "do your own thing" This was, of course, appropriate to the mood of the day which affirmed individual gifts and the courage to venture and use them.

This was a time of great creativity. However, an attendant problem developed. When Christians from a number of congregations gathered, it was difficult to find music that all of them knew and loved. Many local Christian groups were familiar with only a limited collection of songs which might be quite different from that of another group. Only a very few of the new songs were widely known (e.g. "We Are One In The Spirit", "He's Everything to Me"). Thus there was difficulty in such groups singing together.

Black Spirituals could have been useful in providing common materials. However, this was the time of the emotion-laden height of the Civil Rights Movement; the use of such songs was often suspect ("They are condescending or stereotypical"). Common ground could be found only in classic hymnody ("Amazing Grace, "O God Our Help", and, of course, seasonal Christmas and Easter songs).

Today, a great volume of new music is being created - praise choruses for example ("Let's Just Praise The Lord"). Awareness of them is more widespread than was the case in the ventures of the 1960s. However, they too are transient in nature. Classical hymnody can continue to provide a common base of knowledge and experience which transcends songs of the day. Both are needed.

HYMNS CAN BE ECUMENICAL

In many of today's hymnals can be found expressions from the whole family of God without concern for denominational origin. The Christmas section of such a book will be truly ecumenical. Consider how we join with those of other persuasions at Christmas:

"What Child Is This" .... Anglican

"Silent Night" and "O Come All
    Ye Faithful" .... Catholic

"Joy to the World" .... Congregational

"O Little Town of Bethlehem" . . . . Episcopalian

"Away in A Manger" . . . . Lutheran

"Come, Thou Long Expected Jesus and

"Hark, The Herald Angels Sing" . . . . Methodist

"Angels From the Realms of Glory . . . . Moravian

"Let All Mortal Flesh Keep Silence" . . . . Orthodox

"It Came Upon A Midnight Clear" . . . . Unitarian

Nothing about doctrinal differences here. Only the common affirmation that Jesus, God's Son and our Savior is born. Congregations which are intentionally anti-ecumenical unknowingly violate their ecclesiastical position as they sing at Christmas. Second only to the Scriptures, the hymnal can bring all of God's Church together on common ground.

> In its poetry the Church discovers a unity which reaches down below credal differences. The creeds are like the troubled waves on the surface of the waters; the love of which the poets sing is like the undivided ocean below. It is indeed refreshing, as we study our hymnals, to realize that here we can turn aside from controversy and, forgetting our differences, can attain true unity of the spirit in a glad fraternity of praise.[10]

HYMNS CAN BE INTERNATIONAL

This aspect of hymnody needs to be listed here, although it has been dealt with in Chapter 6. The evidence of the coming of Jesus Christ for the salvation of the world is being presented to us through the new hymns from our sisters and brothers of all nations. Nevertheless, in inter-tribal or international gatherings, congregational singing tends to focus on the classic hymns which are known by all.

HYMN
TINKERING

"I don't like that music. I'll change it".

In the proliferation of hymnals today we can see a widespread willingness to redo classic hymns. Some of these changes are made in response to the important concern of articulating the Gospel in a way which includes all persons equally, i.e. "inclusive language". Some represent a desire for modernity - "Get rid of the Elizabethan English". Some are whimsical - "I don't like that particular word or image so I'll change it." Some of those who seek to "fix" the old hymns are ignorant of the way poetic language functions. They are unconcerned about factors of association and memory as they function through the use of symbols. Thus we get "Let's make a new antique". I am not calling all changes into question. Even Charles Wesley approved of altering the line in his hymn from "Hark how all the welkin rings" to "Hark the herald angels sing". I am suggesting that the rationale for any change must be compelling.

Our present-day concern for the use of inclusive language in our worship is a valid one. However, it has brought about the publication of some curious hymns and hymnals. There are problems related to this process.

Part of the difficulty arises from the problem that there is no agreement as to just what inclusive language is. Some say "All language which is not inclusive must be eliminated or changed". What does "inclusive" mean.

Some feel that we must excise all references to God and Jesus which are male-oriented. Thus God as "Father" and Jesus as "Son" are unacceptable (get rid of "This is My Father's World", "Children of the Heavenly Father"). Others would retain these nouns but would eliminate such traditionally male cultural terms as "Lord" and "King" (get rid of "Rejoice, The Lord is King", "Fairest Lord Jesus", "O Come, Let us Adore Him, Christ the Lord"). Still others are uncomfortable only when humanity is referred to in male terms (eliminate "Men and Children Everywhere", "Rise Up O Men Of God", "Good Christian Men Rejoice"). Then, there are many in the Church who don't see any of this as a problem at all.

My objective here is not to attempt to deal with the arguments for or against any of the above positions. Much current literature discussing this is available.[11] Rather, I would like to comment on some of the factors related to changing a hymn text.

First, the attempted rewriting of hymns is not something new. Back in the 1500s, Martin Luther was most unhappy about the altering of his hymns and hymnals as others reprinted them. He wrote that "...there is going to be no end to this haphazard and arbitrary revision which goes on from day to day and that even our first hymns are more and more mutilated with each reprinting." Furthermore, he fears that his hymnal will be "...corrupted and adulterated by blunderheads until the good in it will be lost and only the bad remain." He speaks about how the same thing happened to the writings of Jerome and Augustine and many others. Finally, "In a word [Luther's], there must be mouse dirt with the pepper."[12]

Second, a classic hymn text represents the distillate of generations of hymnological experience. Let us use the example of Charles Wesley. During his ministry (about 1738-1788), he wrote more that 6,500 hymn texts. Only about 250 of these appear in major English-language hymnals of the 20th century. Only 50 are included in the current Methodist hymnal. Thus, more than 6,000 of Wesley's hymns have been discarded. They have not passed the tests by means of which history identifies the timeless and universal.

The figures above illustrate the natural process of attrition that takes place with hymns. Every time a new hymnal is compiled, its editors scrutinize hundreds, even thousands of hymn texts and tunes in the process of deciding which songs to add, which to retain, and which to discard. If a hymn survives this rigorous process across many generations, it has demonstrated that it has remarkable qualities.

Third, only the naive and uninformed believe that it is possible to simply change a few words in a classic hymn without damaging it. Concerning the hymns of Wesley as mentioned above, the small percentage which have survived owe their continuing life to much more than the expression of some particular ideas. Many other subtle factors are involved. These include such things as syllabic rhythm and accent, the smooth or awkward phonating of consonants, the nature of vowel sounds. Other generations have known far better than we about the subtleties of the beautiful use of language. Today it is difficult to find such craftsmanship. We tend to be ill-equipped to do remodeling.

The Authorized (King James) version of Scripture had a linguistic beauty which has not been equaled in subsequent translations. We need newer versions because the primary function of Scripture lies not in its beautiful words but rather in the clarity of its meaning. Hymns are different. Their primary function is not a cognitive one. Rather, they operate in the realm of the emotive. Remember the concept of a "good" hymn as needing to be well sung. Any alteration which diminishes the possibility of delightful singing, no matter how slightly, is destructive.

The inter-relationship of words and music can be seen in the realm of opera. The best composers of opera have always attempted to express through the music the subtle sounds of the text. They have been sensitive to how vowels and consonants are sung, to matters of syllabic accent and rhythm. Of course, when the text of an opera is translated into another language, the fit of text and music will be less satisfying even though acceptable. An opera, however, does not need to survive the regular, repeated editorial process as must a hymn.

Fourth, there are functional problems which arise when a congregation is singing a familiar hymn in which an occasional word has been changed. Many persons will be singing virtually from memory, using the book only for occasional cues. When a new and unexpected word appears some will sing it and others will not. The focus of the singer suddenly shifts. Instead of expressing praise or testimony or commitment, his or her attention is diverted to the change. This may help consciousness-raising but it is certainly not the primary objective of congregational hymn singing. A contemporary hymnologist has suggested that we should consider protecting classic hymns as we do historic buildings.[13]

One must approach the rewriting of classic hymn texts with caution. Any such rewriting must be done only by those who have great skill in the use of language as it is sung.

Consider the relationship of this issue to our present focus of attention. We are suggesting that the use of classic hymns can be a new experience for some congregations. If the traditional language has been altered by inserting contemporary language, we have something which is neither truly old nor new.

IS IT
BIBLICAL?

In the New Testament, there are more than 30 direct quotations from the Psalms, the song book of the Old Testament. There are, many more allusions to their content. Along with the New Testament encouragement of "newness" there is frequent demonstration of the persisting value of the "old".

There is an interesting passage in Deuteronomy 31 which speaks to this concern. There we find recorded a conversation between God and Moses. God is saying that His people, whom Moses is leading, will enter the promised land and there grow fat and comfortable and follow other gods. His word to Moses:

> Now, Therefore, write this song, and teach it to the people of Israel; put it in their mouths, that this song may be a witness for me against the people of Israel...And when many evils and troubles have come upon them, this song shall confront them as a witness (for it will live unforgotten in the mouths of their descendants). [Deut. 31:19, 21]

God will use the ancient songs of His people to bring them back to Himself – but only if they know them.

IS IT
TRADITIONAL?

An interesting phenomenon, visible in many churches today, is the total rejection of all that is not "contemporary" The organ has been replaced by guitars, drums and instrumental tapes. The hymnal has given way to the overhead projector. Classic choral literature has been abandoned in favor of contemporary music for the choir, usually with much unison, many modulations and solos, created for today's mass market.

Traditionally, it has been normative for the Church to use hymns from the past in singing. Even in the 19th century revival meetings of Moody and Sankey, their first collection of Gospel Songs[14] contained 30% of historical hymnody.

It is true that in the sixteenth century Protestant Reformation, virtually all congregational music was new. That was because previously there had been almost no music for the congregation: the choir did the singing. Since that time, it has been customary for the congregation to sing traditional music.

ARE THEY GOOD
TEXTS AND TUNES?

Is an old hymn better than a new one? Probably yes. Any hymn which has survived the culling process for 200 years has demonstrated its universal value. Even as great historical works of art (e.g. the "Mona Lisa") no longer require our judgment to validate their intrinsic value, so classic hymns have demonstrated their value and deserve our serious consideration. These songs are examples of Routley's "well written". True, the text may have been tampered with. The words may have been combined with new experimental tunes. The result of such ventures may be less than "good". However, the original text/tune of classic hymns has been validated by centuries of worshiping Christians.

ARE THEY COMFORTABLE?

Of course not. By nature these classic texts and tunes are more complex than simple gospel songs and choruses. One must engage with them in a learning process. It is good to be able to sing simply "God Is So Good" or "Alleluia". Such songs make no musical or textual demands. They are a brief, obvious, and limited expression of our faith. The Church needs such expressions.

In contrast, consider a stanza from Wesley's "O For A Thousand Tongues":

> Hear Him, ye deaf, His praise ye dumb,
> Your loosened tongues employ.
> Ye blind, behold your Savior come,
> And leap ye lame for joy.

What is this all about? As in all good poetry it may remind us of a number of different things including:

- Jesus' healing miracles;
- The power of God to heal today;

- The ability of spiritual wholeness to transcend physical infirmity;
- The time of Jesus' return when all will be made whole.
- The plight of those who see but do not perceive; hear but do not listen [cf. Isaiah 42:18-20]

All of the above thoughts are caught up in 24 words. However, to process them requires time for reflection. It is unlikely that people think of all these possibilities as the hymn is quickly sung. To gain understanding of them involves a process a bit like that of peeling an onion - layer follows layer as one thinks about what is being expressed and the implications that proceed from such thoughts.

Such a hymn text allows the author to have simultaneous but different conversations with many people. In this way, it can be like the parables of Jesus. In the parable of the Prodigal Son, one reader may identify with the rebellion and repentence of the prodigal, another with the self-righteousness of the elder brother. A third may find challenge in the unqualified joyous acceptance of the father.

Erik Routley wrote a little book dealing with this way of communication. He compares the parabolic process to tossing a ball back and forth. In this analogy, a bit of effort is always involved. There will be some who delight in making the hard catch; others will say "This is too difficult; place the ball in my hands". Routley's comment;

> When [Jesus] spoke publicly he always left something – sometimes a great deal – for the individual mind to do by way of interpretation, amplification and application of what he said.[15]

Singing the simple chorus is like having the ball handed to you. The traditional hymn tends to invite the difficult catch, the creative response.

In my library there are several spice racks holding not spices but tiny hymnals. The books are about three inches high. Most of these pocket hymnals contain words only. Many of them are from the 18th and 19th centuries. They were not meant to be held while singing: they were intended for private devotional study. One could carry them easily, like a pocket Testament.

In times past, people treasured the words of hymns. They studied and memorized them. The words became part of the furniture of their minds. To sing directly from a hymn book was unthinkable. It was felt that songs must come from one's heart rather than being words simply read from the page.[16] This way of understanding a hymn text is related to our present consideration of traditional hymnody.

Engagement with a classic hymn text or tune takes time and attention. Its tune is, by nature, not as immediately accessible as is that of a simple chorus. Its text may require or invite time for reflection before it can be fully appreciated. Praise choruses simply function differently than do classic hymns. Both types can be helpful for the Church. Choruses can provide expression for the newcomer to Christian fellowship. These easy and familiar songs, along with the collection of associations which accompany them, may always have a place in one's singing experience. The classic hymn offers food for those who are growing up into Christ. They meet a different need. You cannot have everything at the same time.

There are congregations whose musical diet consists of the old hymns of the Church. For them, newness might be found in the discovery of some of the rich history and meaning of these familiar materials. Also, fresh ways of combining texts and tunes can bring new life to old songs. More about this in the next chapter.

In summary, exposure to the classic hymnody of the Church may be a new and, sometimes, difficult experience for the congregation. If The nature of these songs is understood, they can be a potent source of memory for the Church. Even as non-Western hymns say "this is what God is doing today", classic hymns say "this is what God has done".

CHAPTER EIGHT

Bringing About Change

How do we bring about change in the church - especially in its worship and music? Our primary concern here is not with kinds of changes we might make. Rather, our focus is on the process involved in making any change. This may be the time to invite you to revisit Chapter 2; to remember the pain, inevitability, biblical nature, and value of change.

ASK "WHY?"
BEFORE "HOW?"

Remember that change in itself is not a valid objective in any enterprise of the church. In an recent encounter with a student of 30 years ago, he said "I move the "Doxology" around to keep the people on their toes". If this is what I taught, I am ashamed; if this is what he perceived, it is unfortunate. Our goal is not to keep people "on their toes". Neither is it to demonstrate how clever we are in the planning of "contemporary" worship. Rather, it is to more effectively open a doorway to God. Simply reshuffling the elements of a worship service will not do this.

When valuable change takes place, it should be the result of a more important concern for something other than change itself. If it results in the congregation being more alert and engaged, great! However, our primary objective is to create a context which might more effectively assist worship "in spirit and in truth".

Newness is not an end in itself. The seeking of newness for its own sake is not only a contemporary problem. Listen to the words of Martin Luther from the 16th century on the creating of new orders of service, new orders of the Mass by many people:

> Some have the best intentions, but, others have no more than an itch to produce something novel so that they might shine before men as leading lights, rather than being ordinary teachers.[1]

Change and newness are not to be feared or avoided. However, it is not enough simply to desire new worship forms for their own sake. There must be a reason for using them which transcends the desire for novelty. They must not be sought as an end in themselves. The pursuit of newness in itself is dysfunctional. It is important that behind every attempt to restructure worship must lie the carefully thought-through conviction that a particular change has the potential of making some aspect of worship more meaningful.

A subtle trap exists for those who plan "creative worship". They easily feel a pressure to make each worship experience different from the one before. An example of this tendency may be seen in conference and convention situations where a number of "model" worship services are displayed. They may or may not be interesting. That's not the point of worship. What is more important they also may or may not be true worship of the living God. God's calling is that worship, even in such a specialized situation, shall find its focus in Him - not in the activity of worship itself, no matter how creative. It is difficult to think about the process and structure of worship and to truly worship at the same time.

Concerning our worship, God calls us (1) to acknowledge and praise Him as creator and Lord of our lives, (2) to look inward re-examining our personal response to His call - our allegiance to God's "worthship", (3) to look around and renew our bonds of commitment with those sisters and brothers who are God's Church, (4) and to look outward to the world which needs to know and recognize Him. Any change should seek to help the worshiping congregation to come closer to one of these objectives.

There are fads in worship as in all other areas of the endeavors of the Church. These may include such things as getting rid of pews, bringing in balloons and requiring all to be joyful, celebrating the Eucharist with coke and potato chips, encouraging all to raise hands in praise. None of these things are bad. All of them emerged in response to an appropriate concern about something that needed changing in worship. However, they are all, in themselves, nothing more than expressions of some felt need. They may not be the fulfilling of that need.

Our problem comes in equating symbols, old or new, with true worship of the living God. Symbols may help but they are not the substance of worship - only possible aids to it. For example, with the medieval icon, the intent was not that one would worship the icon but instead would look through it to the Reality which it represented. Nevertheless the custom arose of venerating the icon itself; this image became the object of worship. The church all too easily tends to cherish the symbol rather than that which it symbolizes. To seize on some contemporary symbol without getting to the reality which it represents is nothing more than faddism. It is appropriate to desire to find new expressions of our faith. We must leave it to time to determine whether such expressions symbolize anything other than a transient fad.

How then do we evaluate such things? To do this, we must first identify the need which is represented by the new expression. Then we must look to Scripture (including parts that we customarily ignore). We should seek wisdom from history. Has the Church had similar needs before? How has it responded to such perceptions? After this, we must seek wisdom from God's Holy Spirit in prayer and dare to trust in what we feel to be His guidance.

UNDERSTANDING
MUST ACCOMPANY CHANGE

Why are we doing this? It may be difficult for worshipers to deal with unexpected change unless they have some understanding of just why the change was introduced. It is always good for them to be reminded from week to week about why they do things, familiar things, in worship. It is ESSENTIAL that they understand why they are being asked to do something different. There are a few rare congregations who have experienced worship as something fluid, governed by other dynamics than the perpetuation of the familiar "liturgy". For such a community the occurrence of the unexpected is not disturbing: it is anticipated. Such congregations are to be envied. The rest of us will need some preparation for change.

Attempt to make the reason for the use of something new clearly self-evident. If this is not possible, then make it a matter of discussion and explanation. Congregations whose worship experience has remained unchanged for a long period of time will not be helped by the sudden inclusion of something new or the exclusion or changing of something predictable and expected. Worshipers will be more acceptant of some innovation in the service if they (a) know that it is going to happen, and (b) understand why it is taking place.

As a simple example, perhaps the pastor/musician wants to use a different tune to sing a familiar hymn text. In the bulletin, under the listing of the name ("Jesus, Lover of My Soul") and page number of the hymn one could simply add "use the tune - Hyfrydol". This reassures the congregation that the organist has not made a mistake. It also introduces the strange word "Hyfrydol" which some might connect with its appearance on the hymnal page.

A few moments might be taken just before the beginning of the service to tell about what is being done and why it might be worthwhile. A paragraph of explanation in the bulletin (not in the order of service itself) can help. The order of service might include no more than the parenthetical line mentioned above. During worship, attention should not be focused on the change itself, but rather on the content of the new experience.

Something new should appear to be obviously appropriate. As an example, I have in mind the rather common situation in which the receiving of the offering is followed by the singing of the Doxology. In this imagined situation these two actions, by this congregation (giving and singing), have always been linked together. Usually, they form a discrete unit, not related in any special way to other worship experiences which precede or follow.

On one morning, let the singing of this expression of praise immediately follow the sermon - not just any sermon but one which focuses on praising God. Let the end of the sermon contain examples of those who praise: affirmations of this activity such as:

> Heb. 2:12, "In the midst of the congregation I will praise Thee"

> Heb. 13:15, "Through him [Jesus] then let us continually offer up a sacrifice of praise to God, that is, the fuit of lips that acknowledge his name"

> Psalm 150:5, "Let everything that breaths praise the Lord. Praise the Lord!"

With no intrusive explanation, let the organist immediately play through the tune (not too fast). This over-familiar hymn, "Praise God From Whom All Blessings Flow" may now invite reflection - more than is usually the case. Have the congregation stand and sing. No further exhortation is necessary. It can be hoped that an unusual readiness will exist to sing in a fresh and meaningful way. No explanation for this different worship experience would be necessary; such explanation would be an intrusion. The very doing of it would reveal its obvious logic.

Preparation for the use of the unusual can take place at many times and in many situations. For example:

A. IN THE SERVICE

As mentioned above, the pastor or worship leader may make some brief comment about a new experience which is to be included in worship. The prelude might be interrupted by a brief explanation of that which is to happen.

There can be information about what is to occur in the bulletin; not in the order of service itself but in an accompanying paragraph of explanation. Scripture may be included which speaks of "newness" ("Sing to him a new song" [Psalm 33:3])

B. AHEAD OF TIME

The meetings of the choir and worship committee can provide opportunity to consider the needs and content of worship. These can be appropriate forums in which to discuss concerns about that which is felt to be lacking in worship and ways in which such deficiencies may be remedied.

New ventures in worship may grow out of a Sunday School class which is focusing on some related subject. An adult or youth group might be considering "Historical Hymnody" - the story of the Church's song in its biblical, historical and contemporary dimensions.[2]

CONNECT
WITH HISTORY

This can reduce anxiety. In this book I have been very intentional in including various historical examples of change, newness, and resistance to such. History can reassure. It can be of help to those in the congregation to know that familiar aspects of worship to which they cling lovingly have been in their own day disturbing to much of the Church.

Conversely, it is reassuring to know that some worship experience which is new for us may be a familiar part of worship in other congregations. Remember the classic prayer for purity of heart which was discussed in Chapter 7. Awareness of its historical linkage can dramatize what it means to be part of the "fellowship of the Saints".

PROVIDE A FAMILIAR,
REASSURING CONTEXT

Change needs to be accompanied by appropriate familiar traditional expressions of faith. An example of this might be the emergence of "pop" music in the church in the 1960s. ALL of the initial ventures into such expression took place in the liturgical church (Catholic, Anglican, Episcopalian, Lutheran). Probably there was heightened motivation as all of these liturgies were made up of old historical familiar materials of worship. More important, when some new musical idiom was introduced (swing, jazz, rock) it was used as a setting for some traditional text such as the Lord's Prayer, a Psalm, the creed, or a classic hymn text or prayer.[3]

The security of the familiar text was always present along with the often-shocking new music.

Within free church worship everything was, by definition, free. The inclusion of radically new music had to stand completely on its own. Widespread use of such nontraditional music did not take place quickly. It was finally accepted only as a tool for evangelism. Ralph Carmichael's evangelical musical "The Restless Ones" was published in 1964. Shortly thereafter, Christian coffee houses, established during the Billy Graham meetings, began to use "pop" music. Only then did the "new" music become accepted by evangelicals as being proper for worship. Initially, such music was thought of as a tool for reaching youth or the inner city with the Gospel. The point here is that in the free church, this new music had to be used without the support of familiar liturgical words. Thus, the shock of introducing "a bit of jazz" into the service was greater.

For our immediate purposes, don't introduce some new element into a worship service and at the same time include an unfamiliar hymn because its content is particularly fitting for the focus of the sermon. Rather, provide a familiar reassuring context. Be intentional about making the materials of the rest of the service things which are comfortable and customary.

THE "NEW"
MUST BE
WELL EXECUTED

Back to the 1960s. The church was exploring the use of new types of contemporary music. Society was affirming the value of "doing your own thing". In a worship service we might have

encountered a junior high school boy or girl who had been per-
suaded to help the congregation with the introduction of some of
the new music. This person might have had a new guitar, a
partial command of two chords, and no sense of rhythm. Such an
experience might have served to affirm the importance and ear-
nestness of the young person involved. It certainly did very little
to encourage the congregation's appreciation of a new musical
idiom.

Perhaps a pastor today might feel the value of introducing a
congregation to the music of Bach. The organist might be a
person of minimal competence; the organ might be one with
foreshortened keyboards and a 10-note pedal board which is rarely
used. It is highly unlikely that some simplified version of a Bach
"classic", played by this person on this instrument will generate
any great appreciation for Bach or make any significant new con-
tribution to worship.

There are available, simple original Bach compositions that
can be played on manuals only.[4] They can represent his style of
music if played with competence and delight.

The point here is that both acceptance of reality, and commitment to unusual effort must characterize any such new endeavor.
"Acceptance of reality" means the making of a realistic appraisal
of resources that are actually available. If such are not within the
congregation and cannot be found within the community, it is
foolish to proceed. A new venture might involve such things as
different music, reordering of the service, introduction of dance
or drama, re-arrangement of the room, use of projected visual
materials. Each of these has its own requirements which must be
met if things are to proceed smoothly and fruitfully.

NEW MUSIC - can it be played or sung by the musicians presently available? Can their interest be enlisted so as to be able to
engage wholeheartedly with it?

REORDERING OF THE SERVICE - Can musicians/worship leaders/ushers be in the proper place at the right time? Are they familiar and comfortable with the changes?

DANCE OR DRAMA - Is appropriate space available? Can all participants be seen or heard? Can appropriate lighting be provided without inviting undue attention to the process?

RE-ARRANGEMENT OF THE ROOM - Can leaders be seen and heard? What problem might be created by sunlight, now coming from a new location? Is congregational movement easy in the new situation? Is there adequate visual contact between singers, director, and instruments? Can ushers function easily? Are necessary hymnals/Bibles/prayer books at hand?

PROJECTED VISUAL MATERIALS - Can the projection surface or screen be adequately darkened without undue fuss? Can the projector be placed and used where it will not be a distraction? Has all necessary equipment been tested in place? Have all materials to be projected been tested in place? Is their brightness satisfactory for the room illumination situation that will be present at the time of the service? Are spare bulbs at hand and does someone present know how to replace them?

The controlling principle should be "KEEP IT SIMPLE AND DO IT WELL!".

CHANGE WILL NOT
ALWAYS BE ACCEPTABLE

We all tend to be uneasy about any change. However, in addition, there are always persons whose reaction to almost everything is negative. They will not hesitate to let you know about their feelings. Do not let a handful of critical responses weigh unduly in your evaluation of the event.

CHANGE
INVOLVES CONSENSUS

Productive change rarely occurs simply because one church leader seeks to initiate it. Significant changes must come out of some kind of group process and decision.

If the pastor is the initiator, he or she must first discuss plans with the church staff or some other leaders. If they cannot be convinced of the necessity or value of the proposed change, it is highly unlikely that the congregation will receive it appreciatively. Also, of course, any such venture will benefit from the thoughts of several people discussing together if they feel that their input is sincerely desired.

There is another more pragmatic reason for needing the involvement of others in this process. As any experienced teacher knows, the "bottom line" is not determined by that which we think we said. Rather, it is the result of that which the listener thinks he or she heard. Interaction between the change-agent and interested others can help to assure that communication really takes place. The leader needs to test his or her ability to share goals and plans.

Beyond this core group whose involvement is of critical importance, there may be other forums in which a proposal for something new could be considered - choir, study group, Sunday School class. A pastor of my acquaintance has the practice of meeting every Thursday with a small group (perhaps half a dozen) to discuss next Sunday's sermon. The composition of the group varies. It may be business men, junior highers, housewives, college students, senior citizens or any similar homogeneous gathering. Something like this could take place with an ad hoc group which comes together to consider a particular worship event. Feedback in such a situation helps to assure that communication takes place - that desired goals and means to reach them are clearly understood.

In such a process there is a dynamic element that must be recognized. When discussion is sought, it must be apparent that the leader (pastor/musician/worship leader) is honestly seeking input, not just ratification of some suggestion. There is an unfortunate tendency of church groups to keep themselves uninvolved. "OK. Go ahead with what you want". That is not enough. We need to seek accountable response such as "Would you recommend this if it were to be presented as your suggestion?"

Dieterich Bonhoeffer has said about this mutuality:

> When one person is struck by the Word, he speaks it to others. God has willed that we should seek and find His living Word in the witness of a brother, in the mouth of man. Therefore, the Christian needs another Christian who speaks God's Word to him. He needs him again and again when he becomes uncertain and discouraged, for by himself he cannot help himself without belying the truth.[5]

What we do concerning church music and, indeed, all of worship is part of our response to God's Word. Bonhoeffer's thoughts about how we perceive this Word are very much to the point.

CHANGE INVOLVES TRUST

The relationship between leader and congregation is a critical element in bringing about any change. The degree of acceptance of any leader will tend to be related to the degree of acceptance of anything new which that leader proposes.

Change often takes place when a new pastor or musician comes upon the scene. This can be dysfunctional if attempted too quickly. The desire to 'make everything new" is dangerous. The new person will be expected to have new ideas, but the congregation will be looking for reassurance that its familiar and comfortable practices will not be abandoned. The incoming leader must seek to affirm as much as possible the things which are accepted as being customary.

Relationships must be established within which new ideas can be explored. Remember that relationships themselves are more important than bringing about change. They must be entered into as something of great value in themselves. They must not be generated simply as a being a tool to bring about a hidden agenda.

In a provocative discussion of this process, R.E.C. Browne has included the comment:

> True influence can only come as a result of relationship, and only where the relationship is not desired in order to exert influence.[6]

Trust must precede change. Such trust will only emerge from the nurturing of honest relationships between church leader and congregation and individuals within it. Any other procedure will be simply a strategy for manipulation.

BE PATIENT!

Normally, changes in any area of life take place slowly. New styles of clothes, hair styling, automobile designs, architecture and home furnishing, all tend do begin with a few venturesome persons and slowly spread. Even more forceful is the bent toward conservatism in the Church. As you venture into changes in worship, considering the suggestions above, allow time for these to be accepted and become comfortable. Above all, be sure that the focus of worship is God, not change.

CHAPTER NINE

Agree to Disagree

This is not a book about rock concerts or opera, country western music or symphonies, jazz or chamber music. Rather, we have been dealing with matters of musical taste insofar as *Christian worship* is concerned. Ultimately, dealing with matters of musical likes and dislikes in this context requires understanding of the nature of the Church. As established in scripture and tradition, the Church is a unique community - God's community. What does He want it to be?

THE NATURE OF
THE CHURCH COMMUNITY

The new Testament gives no explicit, detailed instructions either about how to worship or about what the Church should be. That is why there are so many forms of worship and varieties of "New Testament" churches. Most of the information concerning what the Church should be is offered in the form of images - metaphors. A contemporary theologian has identified ninety-six such images such as "Flock", "People of God", "The New Creation", "The Body of Christ", etc.[1]

The metaphore that the Apostle Paul uses most frequently to describe the Church is that of a body. He refers to the community as "the Body of Christ". This image has three primary facets which are relevant for our consideration.

WE ARE
A DIVERSE GROUP

"...God put every different part in the body just as he wanted it to be. There would not be a body if it were all only one part. As it is, there are many parts but one body." [1 Cor. 12:18-20]

Each of us is unique as far as our abilities and desires. For completeness, we need each other. It is because of this that the matter of relationships was considered in Chapter 8. No one church leader possesses all of the insights and skills that are present in other members of the Body. He or she may be more powerful by virtue of role or personality. He or she may have wider experience or better training. Nevertheless, the Apostle Paul reminds us that he or she cannot take the place of other members of the Body to whom God has given unique gifts. To find the will of God and do His work, we require the contributions of each other.

We will not all agree. Our musical tastes are different; our goals will not all be the same. Our individual experiences will have resulted in understandings and expectations which are not common to each of us at all points. Remember that our diversity is God-given.

The point is that we must work to discover how we can affirm these differences, and how we can learn to work with them. It is a given that we will differ concerning musical matters (and everything else). It should not come as a surprise that some of us like one kind of music, others another. We should not be threatened by this or become defensive. It's OK. We must try to find out how, in one church community, we can put forward our musical needs and, at the same time, affirm other members of the Body whose needs differ from ours.

CHRIST IS
THE HEAD

...we must grow up in every way to Christ who is the head. Under his control all the different parts of the body fit together, and the whole body is held together by every joint with which it is provided. So when each separate part works as it should, the whole body grows and builds itself up through love. [Eph. 4:15,16]

Jesus Christ is meant to be Head of the Body, Lord of the Church. It is as we focus upon Him that we find meaning in our existence and coherence to our variety.

It is easy to find analogies in the physiological arena in which the body or parts of it fail to respond to the control of the head. We may label a situation as "spastic" - one in which the members do not function in appropriate response to the desires of the head.

To recognize Christ's Headship is for all of us to seek His will. We do this, in prayer, in studying Scripture, and in discussion with other members of His Body. Preferences will remain; we try to find out how we can, together, recognize them and work out positive responses.

THE UNITY
OF THE CHURCH

Jesus prayed to God for His Church, saying:

> All I have is yours, and all you have is mine; and my glory is shown through them. And now I am coming to you; I am no longer in the world, but they are in the world. Holy Father! Keep them safe by the power of your name, the name you gave me, so that they may be one even as you and I are one. [John 17:10,11]

"I Did It My Way". This is the essence of original sin - to believe that I don't need God. In the Church, the sin is to feel that my way must determine the musical life of the Body.

The history of the Church offers many examples of congregations which have been troubled, even divided, over musical matters which seem from this distance to have been trivial. The primary question for us should be "What is truly important?"

SEEKING OUR SISTERS' AND BROTHERS' GOOD

The nature of our interrelationship is central. We are a family - a good family where love and concern for one another is shared.

Such sharing may require the relinquishing of some of our personal desires. As members of Christ's Body, each of us, pastor, musician, worshiper, may be called to yield some personal "rights", to abandon some preferences. If something in worship might help others to find God or to grow in their relationship with Him, we are invited to respond with patient acceptance.

C.S. Lewis spoke to this issue as he sought to identify "..the ways in which it {church music] can really be pleasing to God or help to save the souls of men". His outrageous suggestion was that grace would be present when each engaged in the kind of music he or she did not like.

> There can be two musical situations on which I think we may be confident that a blessing rests. One is where a priest or organist [musician], himself a man of trained and delicate taste, humbly and charitably sacrifices his own (aesthetically right) desires and gives the people humbler and coarser fare than he would wish in the belief that he can thus bring them to God. The other is

where the stupid and unmusical layman humbly and patiently, and above all silently, listens to music which he cannot, or cannot fully, appreciate, in the belief that it somehow glorifies God, and that if it does not edify him, this must be his own defect. Neither such a high brow or such a low brow can be far out of the way. To both, church music will have been a means of grace: not the music that they liked but the music that they have disliked. They have both offered, sacrificed their tastes in the fullest sense.[2]

An American pastor expressed the same idea a bit differently:

I know many people who weep at a skilled execution of a Bach cantata but who are not enriched as lovers of persons like me, for instance. They continue to treat me with withering contempt because of my addiction to country music. Have you ever heard "Please, Oh Please Don't Send My Cecil Away"? It will tear your heart out. But it makes classical fans sick and not a little mean-spirited toward us lowbrows. Thus their devotion to beauty does not breed tenderness, affection, or even tolerance. Therefore, whatever else it is, it is not of Christ, who always breeds openness, tenderness, and love.[3]

The Apostle, Paul, in his letter to the Roman church, admonishes us to "Love one another warmly as Christian brothers, and be eager to show respect for one another." [Rom. 12:10]

Erik Routley addressed this problem as he said:

Church music is a pastoral matter. So, if one is asked "What's wrong with that tune?" or "What's wrong with that custom?" one must be able to answer not only in musical terms but in human terms, from ground which is shared with the nonmusical worshipper.[4]

All of the above suggests that an important part of being a member of Christ's Body, the Church, will involve the renunciation of some of one's "rights" for the good of others. The pastor, musician, or worshiper must be willing to set aside some preferences, even to endure some distasteful experiences. In Chapter 3 it was suggested that in order to support our personal prejudices, we tend to develop a rationale for rejecting that which does not please us. Thus, that which offends is criticized as being unbiblical, contrary to our traditions, or unworthy according to our values. These criteria are valid and important but they are all too often misused.

> "We who are strong in the faith ought to help the weak to carry their burdens. We should not please ourselves. Instead we should all please our brothers for their own good on order to build them up in the faith. And may God, the source of patience and encouragement, enable you to have the same point of view among yourselves by following the example of Christ Jesus, so that all of you together may praise with one voice the God and Father of our Lord Jesus Christ. [Romans 15:1,2; 5,6]

It is not essential that we agree on all matters of faith and practice. It is essential that we learn to handle lack of agreement in a Christian manner. Matters of individual preference should not be concealed or ignored. They should be identified and explored in order that mutual growth may take place.

In summary:

If you like the music, enjoy it!

If you don't care for the music - be patient.

Listen! You might come to like it. Someone does.

Endnotes

CHAPTER I -
"THE NATURE OF THE ISSUE"

1. C. S. Lewis. *Letters to Malcolm* (Harcourt, Brace, & World, 1964), pg. 101

2. Gregory Wolfe. "The Church and the Arts: Estranged Bedfellows." p. 24, in *New Oxford Review*, (New Oxford Review, Inc.), June, 1990.

CHAPTER 2 - "CHANGE"

1. C.S. Lewis, *An Experiment in Criticism*, (Cambridge University Press, 1961), p. 17

2. "Troubles connected with the Prayerbook of 1549", *The Camden Miscellany*, (London: John Bowyer Nichols and Son, 1884). p. 141 ff.

3. F.F. Bruce, *The English Bible*. (Oxford University Press, 1961), p. 107

4. Henry Wilder Foote, *Three Centuries of American Hymnody*, (Shoe String Press, 1961) p. 102

5. "Walk To That Glory Land". The Dameans. (F.E.L., n.d.).

6. C.S. Lewis, *George Macdonald, An Anthology*, (The Macmillan Company, 1947), p. 113.

7. Abraham J. Heschel, *Who Is Man?*, (Stanford University Press, 1965), p. 114 ff.

8. Engene Nida, *Message and Mission*, (Harper & Row, 1960), p. 72

9. Archibald Davison, *Church Music, Illusion or Reality*, (Cambridge University Press, 1952), p. 72 ff.

CHAPTER 3 - "WHY DON'T I LIKE SOMETHING DIFFERENT?"

1   Erik Routley, *Is Jazz Music Christian?*, (London: The Epworth Press, 1964), p. 1

2. Wherever the use of music is encouraged in the New Testament, the context is that of communal involvement - no solos or choirs are mentioned. Everyone is to sing. For example:

"Then they sang a hymn and went out to the Mount of Olives". [Matt. 26:30; Mk. 14:26]

"Sing psalms, hymns, and sacred songs". [Col. 3:15; Eph. 5:19]

See also [Rom. 15:9; 1 Cor. 14:14, 26; James 5:13]

3. John Smythe, *The Differences of the Churches of the Separation*, (Amsterdam, 1608), p. 273.

4. Erik Routley, *Into A Far Country*, (Independent Press Ltd., 1962), p. 125 ff.

5. Erik Routley, *Hymns and Human Life*, (Philosophical Library Inc., 1953), p. 299.

6. Karl Barth, *The Knowledge of God*, (Hodder and Stoughton, 1938), p. 179

7. Karl Barth, *Church Dogmatics, Vol. IV, Part 2*, (T. & T. Clark, 1958), p. 867

8. D. W. Whittle, ed, *Memoires of P.P. Bliss.*, (A.S. Barnes & Co., 1877), p. 224

9. Erik Routley, *Christian Hymns Observed*, (Prestige Publications Inc., 1982), p. 106.

10. Roger Hazelton, *A Theological Approach to Art*, (Abingdon Press, 1967) p. 71

CHAPTER 5 - " 'POP' MUSIC AND THE CHURCH"

1. Robert H. Mitchell, *Ministry and Music*, (Westminster Press, 1978), Chapter 8, "Age of Rock or Rock of Ages".

2. Nicolas Slonimsky, *Lexicon of Musical Invective*, (Coleman-Ross Company, 1953), pp. 24-25. Indeed, the whole chapter entitled "Non-Acceptance of the Unfamiliar" is relevant.

3. Some typical examples of the mention of musical instruments in the New Testament are:

   – Matt. 24:31; Rev. 8:7 - 11:15. Angelic trumpets;

   – 1 Cor. 15:52; 1 Thes. 4:16. The last trumpet;

   – Heb. 12:19. Israelites at Sinai.

4. Various instruments are mentioned frequently in the Old Testament; e.g. Psalm 150.

5. The ministry and structure of the Levitical singers is set forth in 1 Chron. 15 and 2 Chron 5.

6. Henry Pleasants, *The Agony of Modern Music*, (Simon and Schuster, 1955), p. 167.

7. Preston Rockholt. *Creative Tensions in Church Music*, (Wheaton College: Scholastic Honor Society, 1969).

CHAPTER 6 - "CHURCH MUSIC FROM THE NON-WESTERN WORLD"

1. *The United Methodist Hymnal*, (United Methodist Publishing House, 1989), uses 46 non-Western texts and/or tunes. It also includes 19 readings/prayers from non-Western cultures.

2. *World Christian Encyclopedia*, ed. David B. Bartlett, (Oxford University Press, 1982).

3. Paul A. Hopkins, *What Next in Mission*, (The Westminster Press, 1977), p. 43.

4. C. Michael Hawn, "A Survey of Trends in Recent Protestant Hymnals: African American Spirituals, Hymns and Gospel Songs.} in *The Hymn*, Vol. 43, No. 1 (The Hymn Society, January 1992), p. 21 ff.

5. "Father, Son and Spirit", found in *C.C.A. Hymnal*, (Christian Conference of Asia, N.C.C., 1963).

6. "Father in Heaven", found in *C.C.A. Hymnal* and *Cantate Domino*, (Oxford University Press, 1980).

7. "Golden Breaks the Dawn", found in *Hymnbook for Christian Worship*, (The Judson Press, 1970).

8. "My Heart Looks in Faith", found in *Baptist Hymnal*, (Broadman Press, 1975), and *Cantate Domino*.

9. "Here O Lord Your Servants Gather", found in *The Presbyterian Hymnal*, (Westminster, 1990), and *The United Methodist Hymnal*, (United Methodist Publishing House, 1989).

10. "He Has Conquered Death", found in *Lead Us Lord*, Howard Olson, (Augsburg, 1977).

11. "Fill Us With Your Love", found in *Fill Us With Your Love and Other Hymns from Africa*, (Agape, 1983).

12. "Enter Into Jerusalem", found in *Sing A New Song* No. 2, Noel Dexter and Paschal Jordan, eds., (The Caribbean Council of Churches, 1977).

13. C. Michael Hawn. "A Survey of Trends in Recent Protestant Hymnals: International Hymnody", in *The Hymn*, Vol. 42 No. 4, (The Hymn Society, Oct. 1991), pg. 24 ff.

CHAPTER 7 - "TRADITIONAL HYMNODY AS 'THE NEW'"

1. Abraham Heschel, *Who Is Man*, (Stanford University Press, 1965), p. 99.

2. The term "Free Church" has two meanings: (1) any church which is free from control by or formal relationship with the State; (2) as used here, any church where the local congregation is free to determine the form and content of worship. e.g. Nazarene, Baptist, Assembly of God. The alternative to "Free Church" is "Liturgical Church". e.g. Episcopalian, Lutheran, Catholic.

3. Bard Thompson, *Liturgies of the Western Church*, (The World Publishing Company 1961). This anthology offers examples of historical liturgies with commentary as to how and when they were developed.

4. This prayer for purity of heart is found in *The United Methodist Hymnal*, 1989; *Lutheran Book of Worship*, 1978;

The Book of Common Prayer, (Episcopal), 1977; etc.

5. Carl Barth, *The Doctrine of Reconciliation Church Dogmatics, Vol. IV, Pt. 2,* tr. by Geofrey W. Bromiley (Edinburgh: T. & T. Clark, 1958), pp. 112 f.

6. James Moffatt, *Handbook to the Church Hymnary, Revised Edition,* (Oxford University Press, 1927), pp. xiv, xx.

7. Williston Walker, *A History of the Christian Church,* (Charles Scribner's Sons, 1959), p. 396.

8. *The Encyclopedia Britanica,* Volume XXVI. Eleventh Edition, (Encyclopedia Britanica, Inc., 1911), p. 856.

9. Albert E. Bailey, *The Gospel in Hymns,* (Charles Scribner's Sons, 1950), pp. 321-328

10. Frederick John Gillman, *The Evolution of the English Hymn,* (London: George Allen & Unwin Ltd., 1927), p. 29.

11. Christopher Idle, *Hymns in Today's Language,* (Grove Books, England, 1982);

    Erik Routley, "Sexist Language: A View From A Distance", in *The Hymn,* Vol. 31, p. 26 ff., (Hymn Society of America, January, 1979;

    Brian Wren, *What Language Shall I Borrow? God-Talk In Worship: A Male Response To Feminist Theology,* (Crossroad Publishing Company, 1989);

    See also prefaces to recent major denominational hymnals

12. "A New Preface by Martin Luther" 1531, in *Luther's Works, Vol. 53,* ed. by Ulrich S. Leupold and Helmut T. Lehmann, (Fortress Press, l965), p. 317 ff.

13. Hugh D. McKellar, " 'In My Memory Locked; or, Change and Decay' ", in *The Hymn,* Vol 43 No. 1, (Hymn Society) p. 47 ff., January, 1992.

14. P.P. Bliss and Ira Sankey, *Gospel Hymns and Sacred Songs,* (John Church & Co. 1875).

15. Erik Routley, *Into A Far Country,* (Independent Press, London, 1962), Chapter 1. "The Principle of Trajectory".

16. In England in the beginning of the 1600s, Baptist pastor John Smythe said about congregational singing "I hold it unlawful to hold the book before the eyes while singing." One must sing from the heart. Quoted in "Spiritual Worship in Baptist Churches", Judson LeRoy Day, (*Foundations*, July- Sept. 1971), p. 268).

CHAPTER 8 - "BRINGING ABOUT CHANGE"

1. Martin Luther's Preface to his German Mass of 1526. *Luther's Works, Vol. 5,* ed. by Ulrich S. Leupold and Helmut T. Lehman. Philadelphia: Fortress Press, 1965, p. 61

2. As a suggested teacher's text consider Eskew and McElrath's *Sing With Understanding,* (Broadman Press, 1980), or, if a copy could be found, Albert Bailey's *The Gospel in Hymns,* (Charles Scribner's Sons, 1950).

3. Some recorded examples of such experiments are:

   "20th Century Folk Mass" by Geofrey Beaumont. Frank Weir and the Peter Knight Singers, (Fiesta Records, c. 1958).

"Liturgical Jazz", Ed Summerlin and Roger Ortmayer, at Southern Methodist University. 1959.

"Missa Luba", Congolese, Father Hazen, 1958.

"American Jazz Mass", Frank C. Tiro, n.d.

"Missa Criolla", Ariel Ramirez, (Lawson-Gould Music, 1963).

"Rejoice", Herbert G. Draesel, et. al., (Marks Music, 1965), done for General Theological Seminary, N.Y.

4. Such simple Bach compositions for two hands, without pedal might be:

"Aria" from *Notenbuchlein fur Anna Magdelina Bach.*

"Wer Nur den Lieben Gott Lasst Walten" ("If Thou But Suffer God To Guide Thee") from *Clavier-Buchlein vor W.F. Bach.* also "Nun Komm Der Heiden Heiland" (Now Come, Savior of the Heathen"), "Gottes Sohn Ist Kommen" (God's Son Has Come").

5. Dieterich Bonhoeffer, *Life Together*, (S.C.M. Press Ltd. 1949), p. 12 ff.

6. R.E.C. Browne, *The Ministry of the Word*, (S.C.M. Press, Ltd., 1958), p. 120.

CHAPTER 9 - "AGREE TO DISAGREE"

1. Paul S. Minear. *Images of the Church in the New Testament*, (Westminster, 1960).

2. C.S. Lewis, "On Christian Music", in *Christian Reflections*, ed. by Walter Hooper, (Wm. B. Eerdmans Publishing Company, 1967), p. 94,

3. Norman R. DuPuy from "Is Nothing Sacred", *The American Baptist*, (The American Baptist Churches in the U.S.A.), May 1975.

4. Erik Routley. *Music Leadership in the Church*, (Agape, 1984).